GREAT AMERICAN ENTREPRENEURS

Henry Ford

Assembly Line and Automobile Pioneer

Gerry Boehme

Cavendish Square

New York

Published in 2020 by Cavendish Square Publishing, LLC
243 5th Avenue, Suite 136, New York, NY 10016

Copyright © 2020 by Cavendish Square Publishing, LLC

First Edition

Website: cavendishsq.com

This publication represents the opinions and views of the author based on his or her
personal experience, knowledge, and research. The information in this book serves as a general
guide only. The author and publisher have used their best efforts in preparing this book and
disclaim liability rising directly or indirectly from the use and application of this book.

All websites were available and accurate when this book was sent to press.

Library of Congress Cataloging-in-Publication Data

Names: Boehme, Gerry, author.
Title: Henry Ford : assembly line and automobile pioneer / Gerry Boehme.
Description: First edition. | New York : Cavendish Square, 2020. | Series: Great
American entrepreneurs | Includes bibliographical references and index.
Identifiers: LCCN 2018050343 (print) | LCCN 2018053802 (ebook) | ISBN 9781502645357 (ebook) |
ISBN 9781502645340 (library bound) | ISBN 9781502645333 (pbk.)
Subjects: LCSH: Ford, Henry, 1863-1947. | Industrialists--United States--Biography. |
Automobile industry and trade--United States--History--Juvenile literature. |
Businesspeople--United States--History--Juvenile literature.
Classification: LCC HD9710.U52 (ebook) | LCC HD9710.U52 B64 2020 (print) |
DDC 338.7/629222092 [B] --dc23
LC record available at https://lccn.loc.gov/2018050343

Editorial Director: David McNamara
Editor: Kristen Susienka
Copy Editor: Rebecca Rohan
Associate Art Director: Alan Sliwinski
Designer: Joseph Parenteau
Production Coordinator: Karol Szymczuk
Photo Research: J8 Media

The photographs in this book are used by permission and through the courtesy of: Cover, Stock Montage/
Archive Photos/Getty Images; pp. 4, 47, 53, 62, 71, 78, 81, 88 Bettmann/Getty Images; p. 7 Imran's Photography/
Shutterstock.com; p. 8 Universal History Archive/UIG/Getty Images; p. 15 William L. Sheppard/Library of
Congress/File: First use of the Cotton Gin, Harper's weekly, 18 Dec. 1869, p. 813.png/Wikimedia Commons/
Public Domain; p. 19 Radnorimages/Alamy Stock Photo; pp. 22-23 Photo12/UIG/Getty Images; p. 26 Staff/
Mirrorpix/Getty Images; p. 32 Keystone Features/Getty Images; pp. 34-35 Unknown/Archive.org/File: Henry
Ford and Barney Oldfield with Old 999, 1902.jpg/Wikimedia Commons/Public Domain; p. 37 Apic/Getty
Images; p. 39 Cullen328, Own work/File: 1909 Ford Model T advertisement.jpg/CCA-SA 3.0 Unported;
pp. 42-43 Herbert Gehr/The LIFE Images Collection/Getty Images; p. 50 Fotosearch/Getty Images; p. 57
Buyenlarge/Getty Images; p. 64 George Rinhart/Corbis/Getty Images; p. 74 Pierre Poschadel, Own work/File:
Paris (75), musée des Arts et métiers, Ford model T, 1908 1.jpg/Wikimedia Commons/CCA-SA 3.0 Unported;
p. 90 Applesnonions, Own work/File: Greenfield Village, Liberty Craftworks 1.jpg/CCA-SA 3.0 Unported;
p. 92 Clari Massimiliano/Shutterstock.com; p. 97 Hulton Archive/Getty Images; p. 99 © Wally McNamee/
Corbis/Getty Images; p. 103 photo-denver/Shutterstock.com; p. 104 Rebecca Cook/Reuters/Newscom.

Printed in the United States of America

CONTENTS

INTRODUCTION ... 5
Automobiles for Everyone

ONE ... 9
Turbulent Times

TWO ... 27
A Lifelong Commitment to Improvement

THREE ... 51
Predecessors, Partners, and Competitors

FOUR ... 65
Historical Accomplishments

FIVE ... 79
Shaped By His Era

SIX ... 93
Driving New Directions

Chronology / 106

Glossary / 108

Sources / 111

Further Information / 118

Bibliography / 120

Index / 125

About the Author / 128

Automobiles for Everyone

H enry Ford was born on July 30, 1863, on a small family farm located just outside of Detroit, Michigan. Once he became an adult, the world would never be the same.

Fashioning an Entrepreneur

One of the most influential business entrepreneurs in US history, Henry Ford changed the way Americans worked, how they drove, and how they lived. While still a teenager, Ford abandoned his traditional way of life to become an industry icon, in many ways mirroring the broad transition taking place in the United States during the rise of the Industrial Revolution.

Henry Ford (*center*) proudly drives his revolutionary Model T with friends John Burroughs (*left*) and Thomas Edison (*right*).

The American Civil War ended just two years after Ford's birth. While the North's victory over the South ended slavery and preserved the union, it also marked the beginning of a new industrial era in the United States. The steam engine helped drive this revolution, powering railroads, farm machinery, and even the first "horseless carriages."

The course of Henry Ford's career followed a similar path. Since early childhood, Ford had exhibited strong interest in machinery, whether it was tinkering with mechanisms for clocks and watches, or repairing steam-powered machines on his farm. Ford hated the fact that only wealthy people could afford modern conveniences, and he imagined how he might use technology to make life better for ordinary citizens.

In 1876, Ford was riding a horse-drawn carriage when he saw a cart driving along a local road. It was moving by steam power. Most people back then used horses to get from place to place, or they simply walked. By many accounts, that may have been the moment when Ford decided to spend his life building self-powered vehicles.

Leaving a Legacy

Throughout his career, Ford's farming background continued to influence his pursuit of efficient production, and he strove to improve people's mobility and lifestyle. Unlike other carmakers at that time, Henry Ford wasn't interested in manufacturing automobiles for wealthy buyers. He wanted to build an affordable car for everyone. Ford's Model T allowed him to finally accomplish his vision, producing a cheap, reliable car that everyone could own.

In addition to the Model T, Henry Ford's many notable accomplishments include the modern assembly line, the eight-

The company that Henry Ford founded more than one hundred years ago remains one of the largest and most successful automobile manufacturers today. The distinctive Ford logo has changed little since it first appeared in the early 1900s.

hour workday, and higher pay for his employees. Despite his success, however, Ford was also a man of contradictions. Early conflicts with his financial backers caused him to increasingly rely on his own opinions and to mistrust any outside advice. This caused problems, both at his company and with his family. Later in life, Ford was also accused of bigotry, and he resisted workers' efforts to unionize.

Henry Ford left a complex legacy that continues to fascinate historians today. Author Russ Banham wrote that, "Henry Ford is so complex and so elusive that one hundred biographies have tried to delineate his character, shedding light on his facets while obscuring the whole."[1]

Famous author and humorist Will Rogers, who lived during Henry Ford's time, described Ford's influence much more simply: "It will take a hundred years to tell if [Ford] helped us or hurt us, but he certainly did not leave us where he found us."[2]

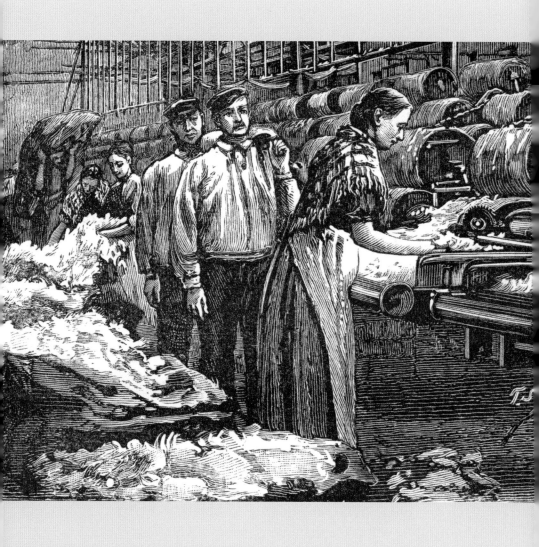

CHAPTER ONE

Turbulent Times

Henry Ford was born in 1863, a very difficult year for the United States. Just eighty-seven years after declaring independence from Great Britain and nearly seventy-five years after adopting the US Constitution, the young country was literally being torn apart.

Clear Divisions

From 1861 to 1865, America's Civil War pitted Northern states against Southern states in a savage battle over monumental issues. Chief among them were slavery and balancing power between state and federal governments. Former friends became bitter enemies as the nation

The Industrial Revolution fueled the growth of mass-produced goods made in factories like the late nineteenth–century textile mill shown here.

plunged into a war that split families and threatened to dismember the fragile union. By the time Ford was born, the struggle had already consumed two long years, with no clear end in sight.

While slavery and states' rights certainly framed the conflict, the Civil War also marked an even wider historical turning point. American lives were changing and had been for some time. The pace of that transformation was now increasing, and the conflict between the Northern and Southern states brought to the forefront an even broader distinction between what had become two radically different Americas.

Industrial Revolution

This period of change in America took place during what we now call the Industrial Revolution, a historical period that stretched out more than a century, and which significantly changed the world and its people forever. Historians describe it as a time when societies around the world experienced unprecedented economic and social changes, driven for the most part by rapid development of new technologies. Interestingly enough, it all began in America's former mother country, Great Britain.

Built in Britain

The Industrial Revolution received its kick-start in Great Britain in the late 1700s, and it happened for a number of different reasons. The American colonies had successfully broken away to form their own nation by 1783, but Great Britain remained a dominant world power with a stable government and an extensive empire that spanned the globe. The British population was growing due to strong agriculture and a healthy environment, especially for that time, and more people were now looking for jobs beyond the farm.

Great Britain also claimed abundant natural resources that helped build industry. Coal and iron provided energy and materials for manufacturing, and England's rivers furnished both a means of transportation and an important power source. Great Britain's foreign colonies supplied a wealth of raw materials, while their settlers and native populations constituted a growing consumer market for finished goods being produced back home.

Just as important, Britain's society had evolved to create a strong sense of social mobility; its citizens believed that hard work and creativity could lead to higher social status and increased wealth. Given that British inventors also tended to concentrate on practical applications of technology and science, the combination of resources, entrepreneurship, and technology left the nation well poised to start an economic revolution.

More and Better

As England's population grew and markets expanded, merchants looked for ways to produce goods more quickly and with higher quality. Textiles, for instance, grew to become one of Great Britain's most important industries. In the mid-to-late 1700s, new machines were being developed to help in the textile-making industry. Inventors like Edmund Cartwright helped mechanize the process of weaving thread into cloth.

Improvements in iron production also played a key role in boosting British manufacturing capabilities. Abraham Darby discovered a cheaper and easier method to produce cast iron; Henry Bessemer developed the first inexpensive process for mass-producing steel. Iron and steel became essential materials, used to make everything from appliances, tools, and machines to ships, buildings, and factories.[1]

Powered by Steam

Among all the development happening at the time, perhaps nothing ranked higher in importance than the evolution of steam engines. Steam could power the machines that made factories run. Steam engines were also portable, which meant that factories no longer needed to be located near rivers that supplied their energy. Steam could also drive the ships and trains that moved people and goods more quickly and efficiently, slowly but surely replacing the sailing ships and horse-drawn carts that people had depended on for centuries.

In the early 1800s, British engineer Richard Trevithick constructed the first railway steam locomotive. In 1830, England's Liverpool and Manchester Railway became the first to offer regular passenger services. In the early 1800s, American Robert Fulton built the first commercially successful steamboat, and by the mid-nineteenth century, steamships were carrying freight across the Atlantic Ocean.[2]

Made in the USA

When British colonists first came to America, they were much more interested in farming the vast tracts of available land than working in factories like those that were springing up back home. It wouldn't take long, however, before Great Britain's technological breakthroughs made their way across the Atlantic to America.

Late in the 1700s, Samuel Slater and other entrepreneurs started the first American cotton mills in Massachusetts, using technology from Great Britain. As these and other types of small businesses expanded, craftsmen usually produced small amounts of goods in their own homes, then sold them to those nearby or to local merchants.

Bigger Scale

As demand for products expanded, creative business managers began to join individual households together to form a kind of network called an "outwork system," where homes produced smaller parts that were then collected and assembled into complete products. This idea quickly expanded to factories, where workers produced complete goods in a single location. Among the early innovators of this approach were a group of businessmen known as the Boston Associates, who recruited thousands of New England farm girls to operate machines in their new factories.[3]

Mirroring the early development that took place in Great Britain, the first American manufacturers also used nearby rivers or streams for power and transportation. Later, as the pace and scope of production expanded, new and better methods began to emerge in America as well, including steam engines and railroads, and boats traveling on rivers, lakes, and canals.

New Funding Sources

In order to expand their businesses even further, manufacturers began to seek out investors and bank loans so they could have access to money to add machinery and hire more workers. Governments now assumed a greater role, both in supporting new banking institutions as well as helping to build better transportation networks. In 1825, for example, New York State completed the Erie Canal to connect the Atlantic Ocean to the Great Lakes. In 1837, the federal government finished a 620-mile (998-kilometer) national road from Maryland to Illinois to help move people and goods to the West.

As American industry continued to expand, another equally important shift began to emerge. In this case, however, the signs of disruption were subtler, and it would take decades before the true effects would come to light. From the 1830s to 1860s, the United States was beginning to split into two distinct halves, dividing the industrial northeast from the agricultural south.

Factories or Farms

The Industrial Revolution initially took root in America's northeast, in part due to simple geography. New England's hilly land and harsh climate did not suit agriculture very well. Its people had congregated in towns and cities looking for work, and its minerals and rivers were better suited to supporting manufacturing than farms.

Southern states, on the other hand, boasted vast farmland, and their climate supported all kinds of agriculture, including important crops like tobacco and cotton. Just as crucially, the institution of slavery provided wealthy Southern plantation owners with a free source of labor to work their fields and bring their products to market.

Strangely, while manufacturing capability expanded much more readily in the North than the South, the Industrial Revolution actually led to the development of technology that also helped to reinforce the agrarian economy of the plantation states. In a larger sense, the Industrial Revolution helped to maintain conditions that resulted in the Civil War.

Whitney's Invention

Perhaps the war would never have come about had certain technology not been invented. In the late 1700s, the Southern plantation system was close to collapse. Products like cotton yielded less and less profit. Cotton fiber had to be picked and separated from its seeds by hand. This was a long and difficult process. While owners did not pay their slaves, they were still expensive to maintain. Low production and high costs threatened to put many Southern plantations out of business.

This 1869 illustration from *Harper's Weekly* depicts slaves working on a cotton plantation. New machines like Eli Whitney's cotton gin helped support Southern plantations and slavery by increasing agricultural production and reducing costs.

In 1794, however, Eli Whitney patented his cotton gin (short for "engine"), a machine that made it easier and faster to remove seeds from cotton fiber. Cotton could now be produced much more quickly and efficiently, and it began to generate huge profits, both for growers as well as textile mills located both in the American northeast and in Great Britain. By the mid-nineteenth century, cotton had risen to become America's leading export and had totally turned around the Southern economy.

The cotton gin allowed Southern states to maintain their agricultural roots even as Northern cities grew due to the expansion of manufacturing. Unfortunately, the higher demand for cotton had tragic human consequences. While Northern states had outlawed slavery by 1820, Southern plantation owners now relied more than ever on the slave trade. This dependency contributed to tilting the balance toward civil war forty years later, and ultimately resulted in a contest for the union, which ended in 1865.

Peace Accelerates Industrialization

When the Civil War finally ended, the technological revolution that had come to America more than fifty years earlier now helped the country to recover and grow. During the war, much of America's manufacturing capability focused on producing the tremendous amounts of guns, ammunition, uniforms, wagons, and trains that armies used to outfit their soldiers and fight their battles. When the war ended, this industrial capacity quickly converted to manufacturing the products of peace.

The Library of Congress describes the new age that began for American industry:

Following the Civil War, industrialization in the United States increased at a breakneck pace. This period, encompassing most of the second half of the nineteenth century, has been called the Second Industrial Revolution or the American Industrial Revolution. Over the first half of the century, the country expanded greatly, and the new territory was rich in natural resources. Completing the first transcontinental railroad in 1869 was a major milestone, making it easier to transport people, raw materials, and products.[4]

On the Move

The transcontinental railroad served to unite the nation by enabling people and goods to move more easily from one coast to the other. Technology also helped fuel growth in agriculture and migration. Railroads helped open up the great corn and cattle lands of the American West, and hundreds of thousands of settlers moved there, many of them immigrants from Europe. Between 1860 and 1900, fourteen million immigrants came to the country—some to work on farms, while others took jobs in an array of industries, including railroads and city factories.

Inventors and Tycoons

It was an exciting time to live in America. During the 1870s, inventors like Alexander Graham Bell and Thomas Alva Edison developed and perfected many different technologies that helped people live, communicate, and travel better than before, including the lightbulb, the telegraph, and the telephone. New processes like open-hearth steel production

FORD'S GAS ENGINE

Steam engines helped power the Industrial Revolution, so it seemed natural for inventors to try and harness steam to drive early versions of self-propelled vehicles. Henry Ford originally wanted to build steam-powered tractors for farmers, but he quickly realized that steam engines were too heavy and dangerous for everyday use.

He began to read about German inventors like Nikolaus Otto, Gottlieb Daimler, and Karl Benz. They had built "internal combustion" engines in the 1860s that mixed gasoline with air, then compressed the mixture inside a small closed space called a cylinder. When they ignited this mixture, the resulting explosion moved a small metal piece called a piston, which could then be used to power a machine or a vehicle.

Ford began to experiment by building his own gas engine in a workshop behind his house, using scrap metal for parts. On Christmas Eve 1893, he moved his engine into the kitchen to test it, running a wire from an electric light in the ceiling to ignite the fuel. His wife Clara fed gasoline as Ford sparked the engine. When it sputtered to life, Ford knew he had found a source of power for his horseless carriage.

Internal combustion engines have come a long way since Henry Ford experimented with his "kitchen engine" in 1893.

made it possible to make high-grade steel faster and cheaper. Networks of oil pipelines made it easier to move the fuel source from wells that pumped it from the ground to factories that used its power.

The age also helped create a new breed of American industrialists who had bold visions and took aggressive steps to build their businesses. For example, during this period of rapid change, Andrew Carnegie established the first steel mills in the United States to use the British "Bessemer process" for mass-producing steel. Carnegie also strove to control every aspect of the steelmaking process, including the mines that produced the raw material for steel, the mills and ovens that created the final product, and the railroads and shipping lines that transported the goods.

Other industrialists like John D. Rockefeller merged the operations of many large companies to form trusts. Rockefeller's Standard Oil Trust eventually grew to control 90 percent of the oil industry, severely limiting competition.

Abuse of Economic Power

All this growth did not come without a cost, however. These industrial monopolies were often accused of intimidating smaller businesses and competitors in order to maintain high prices and profits. Industrial leaders also used their wealth to gain political clout, pushing the US government to adopt policies that promoted industrial development at the expense of ordinary people. For example, the government worked with businesses to provide land for the construction of railroads and maintain high tariffs to protect American industry from foreign competition.[5]

Describing the effects of these times, blogger Rebecca Beatrice Brooks writes:

> The lack of government regulation allowed businesses to flourish and grow at a rapid pace. Business owners had full control of their companies without government interference. Although this was good for business, it created widespread environmental problems and poor working conditions.[6]

Beginnings of Urbanization

In retrospect, the rise of industry after the Civil War marked the beginning of America's transition from a rural society to an urban one. Despite the hardships of factory work, young people raised on farms saw greater job opportunities in larger cities. They began to head toward the factories, as did millions of immigrants. In 1800, only 6 percent of the population of America lived in cities. By 1900, that number had increased to 40 percent, and by 1920, the majority of Americans lived in cities.[7]

A Farmer's Son

Like many farm boys around his age, Henry Ford grew up to have the same vision. Ford was born on his family's farm about 9 miles (15 km) outside Detroit, Michigan, in 1863. Like most farming families at that time, the Fords grew crops like wheat and vegetables and also raised animals, including pigs, cows, and horses.

Ford spent his childhood doing hard, physical work; for the most part, new technology that had started to improve

As shown in this 1900 photograph of Fifth Avenue in New York City, early self-powered vehicles were few and far between, and they were convincingly outnumbered on city streets by horse-drawn carriages. However, by the end of the Great Depression and World War II, automobiles had replaced horses as the primary means of transportation in the United States.

manufacturing and transportation in the United States had not yet found its way to the typical American family farm. While Ford's father did use horse-drawn machinery, most farmers still did things by hand. Only the most well off could afford to use expensive, steam-powered machines to help them grow and harvest their crops.

Henry Ford hated the monotony and wasted time of farm life, and from an early age he imagined how machines might make his life better. He once wrote, "I have followed many a weary mile behind a plow and I know all the drudgery of it. What a waste … when in the same time a tractor could do six times as much work."[8]

Seeing the Future

Detroit was already beginning to come into its own as a manufacturing center during Ford's childhood. Its location along the Great Lakes and its position as a railroad hub helped Detroit become an important transportation center. Nearby raw materials included lumber, copper, and salt deposits. They helped the city become a leader in the new but rapidly growing chemical industry.

In his book *Ford: The Times, the Man, the Company*, biographer Allan Nevins describes how Henry Ford witnessed the growth of industry while still a young boy on his family farm:

> As Henry Ford entered childhood just after the Civil War, he could sometimes see on the horizon to the southeast a haze made by the heavy smoke of the freighters constantly passing between Lake Erie to the south and Lakes St. Clair and Huron on the

north; he could see to the east the faint but ever-denser smudge of Detroit's numerous small mills, factories, and machine shops. Even his small town, Dearbornville, already had a sawmill, flour mills and an iron foundry.[9]

Henry Ford was beginning to see the future. It was only several miles away, and it seemed a natural fit with his own growing interest in efficiency and machines.

CHAPTER TWO

A Lifelong Commitment to Improvement

I f we could travel back in time to Henry Ford's childhood world, it would be hard to predict that he would one day become one of the most influential business leaders in US history.

A Difficult Start

The oldest of six children, Ford spent his formative years living the hard life of the mid-1800s American farmer. Early each morning, he rose and joined his brothers and sisters, milking cows, plowing land, and performing other chores to help his parents. Ford's father, William, had immigrated to the United States from Ireland in 1847, looking for cheap land. After marrying Ford's mother,

Henry Ford credited his wife Clara (*left*) as his greatest supporter.

Mary, in 1861, the couple settled in their seven-room farmhouse to build a life and raise a family.

The Ford farm may have only been a few miles from the city of Detroit, Michigan, but for Ford and his family, it may as well have been on a different planet. Most people at that time either rode horses or walked to get from one place to another. Trips to nearby villages or even to visit neighbors could be difficult or dangerous. Many rural families spent most of their time isolated on their own farms, with little contact beyond their own local schools, churches, and towns.

Practical Learning

Ford began attending South Settlement School when he was seven years old. All the students sat in a single room with only one teacher. They learned about typical school subjects, but also about morality and proper public behavior. Henry Ford was not a great student; biographer Carin Ford wrote that "Henry was good at reading and arithmetic, but he never learned to spell or write clearly. All his life, writing even a simple sentence was hard for him."[1] Ford only completed school up to the sixth grade, but he did enjoy learning about things he was interested in. He particularly liked watching workers who operated and built machines, and he appreciated being taught by people who actually did the job.

Passion for Machines

Around the same time that Ford started school, a worker on the family farm took apart his watch to show him how it ran. That lesson sparked his lifelong interest regarding how intricate parts could be manufactured and assembled to make useful tools. Regardless of what it was—a clock to tell time, a toy to entertain young children, or a machine to make work easier—Ford enjoyed them all.

He began to learn everything he could about watches. He fashioned his own tools from bits of metal he found around the house and examined any watch he could find. One of his neighbors once said that "every clock in the Ford home shuddered when it saw him coming."[2]

Ford also liked to disassemble toys to see how they worked, and his two sisters and three brothers tried to hide their playthings from him. "When we had … toys given to us at Christmas," remembered one sister, "we always said, 'Don't let Henry see them! He'll take them apart.'"[3]

Henry's interest in machinery soon sparked his curiosity in other things he saw around the house. According to one story, Ford once saw steam rising from a pot of boiling water and wondered what would happen if he blocked the steam from escaping. After he covered the pot, the building pressure soon caused it to explode. Ford came away impressed by how compressed steam could provide so much power.

A Mother's Influence

By all accounts, Ford's father was a stern taskmaster. He believed that children should work on the farm just as hard as their parents. Ford's mother Mary was a more loving influence, but she also stressed the importance of hard work, discipline, and proper behavior. "You must earn the right to play," she once said. "The best fun follows a duty done."[4]

Tragically, Henry Ford lost his mother when he was just twelve years old. Mary Ford died shortly after giving birth to the couple's eighth child, who was stillborn. William and Mary

Ford had also lost their first child, who had only survived a few days before dying.

Ford was devastated when his mother died, and he expressed his sorrow in words that reflected his growing fascination with machines. With his mother gone, Ford said, "The house was like a watch without a mainspring."[5]

After his mother died, Ford continued to work on the farm, but he hated the daily tedium and repetitive tasks that filled his day. "What a waste of time it is for a human being to spend hours and days behind a slowly moving team of horses," Ford thought.[6] As he became more interested in machines, he began to imagine how he might use this new technology to improve life on the farm.

Lasting Impression

In 1876, Ford saw something on a Michigan dirt road that changed his life. In those days, most people still used horse-drawn carriages or wagons for transportation. Bicycles had started to appear in the cities, but they were expensive, in short supply, and not well suited for the rough paths and trails of America's rural areas. Farmers sometimes used steam engines to power the equipment in the field, but even then the owners usually had horses pull their machines from one place to the other.

On this particular day, Ford was riding with his father when they suddenly came upon a cart that appeared to be moving under its own power. A large steam engine sat on the back of the cart, and someone had connected a chain from the engine to the cart's wheels. Ford jumped off his wagon to study this fascinating contraption and ask how it worked. Some historians believe that he decided right then and there to spend his life building these self-powered vehicles.

On the Move

In 1879, at the age of sixteen, Henry Ford decided to leave the family farm and move to Detroit to pursue his interest in machinery. His father tried to talk him out of it, but he had learned that when his son decided to do something, it was difficult to change his mind. Others would soon learn that lesson too.

Ford soon got a job at the Flowers Brothers Machine Shop, where he helped make fire hydrants, pipes, and other items from brass and iron. He also worked at a jewelry store repairing clocks and watches and began to read articles in technical magazines like *Scientific American* and *World of Science*. Ford later attended a business school, where he studied bookkeeping, business, and mechanical drawing. While he got the chance to work on steam engines at the shop, he also learned about new internal combustion engines that ran on a fuel called gasoline.

In 1882, he moved back home to work for a neighboring farmer named John Gleason. Gleason owned a steam engine, which he put on a wagon and rented to local farmers to run their woodchoppers and other equipment. Henry carted the engine to the area's farms and became responsible for its operation and repair. The more he worked with these large, heavy, and inefficient machines, the more Ford believed that the days of steam power were coming to an end, and that internal combustion engines would rule the future.

Meeting His Match

It was during his time back on the farm that Henry Ford met a young woman named Clara Bryant at a local dance. Clara was nineteen years old, three years younger than Ford, and lived on a nearby farm with her nine brothers and sisters. Later in life, Ford said that he knew almost immediately that Clara was the right woman for him.

Ford and Clara soon became engaged and were married on April 11, 1888, Clara's twenty-second birthday. While they didn't always agree, Clara usually supported Ford's desires over her own and consistently told him he would be successful no matter what. Henry Ford once said of his wife, "It was a very great thing to have my wife even more confident than I was."[7]

Illuminated

After their marriage, Ford's father gave the couple a small plot of land for them to farm. Ford soon built a small shed where he could continue to experiment with internal combustion engines. Three years later, in 1891, Ford announced that he and Clara would be moving to Detroit so he could pursue his love of machines and technology full time. Clara did not want to leave her new house and the farm, but she still agreed to go.

When he arrived in Detroit, Ford got a job at the Edison Illuminating Company. At that time, famous inventor and businessman Thomas Edison owned several companies that provided electricity to cities around the United States. Ford was looking for a better way to ignite the mixture of gasoline and air in his internal combustion engine, and he thought that electricity might provide some answers.

While Ford spent much of his time at Edison repairing huge steam engines that provided electricity for Detroit, he also managed to work on a small gas engine that he hoped could power his first horseless carriage, an early popular term that described what came to be known as automobiles.

SELFLESS DEVOTION

Ford always credited two women as playing central roles in influencing his life. One was his mother Mary. The other was his wife Clara. "The greatest day of my life was the day I married Mrs. Ford," he once said. When Clara first met Ford at a local dance, she liked his serious nature and intensity, and enjoyed talking with him about his business ideas and dreams. For his part, Ford described his wife as the "great believer" who always supported his passions and work.[8] According to one description, Clara "brought common sense, a charitable spirit, energy and enthusiasm to Henry's many pursuits and her own extensive activities."[9]

While Clara usually supported Ford's plans, she could also firmly resist him when she thought he was wrong. She later played an important role in forcing him to accept unions in Ford plants and installing his grandson, Henry II, as president of Ford.

Clara passed away in 1950, three years after her beloved husband.

Henry and Clara Ford sit in the first Ford car ever made, built in 1896.

Ford (*right*) built racing cars to attract attention. He hired Barney Oldfield (*seated*) to drive his famous 999 racer, which he named after a famous steam locomotive that set a 112-mile-per-hour (180 kmh) speed record in 1893.

Ford began to use his bold vision of self-powered vehicles and his powers of persuasion to convince other machinists, designers, and engineers to help him, and he soon gained the reputation of

someone who might accomplish big things in life. One of his early partners, mechanic Fred Strauss, remembered, "Henry had some kind of 'magnet.' He could draw people to him."[10]

Edsel Arrives

On November 6, 1893, Clara gave birth to their first and only child, Edsel. The Fords named him after Ford's childhood friend Edsel Ruddiman, who later became a scientist and married Ford's sister Margaret. Ford took great pride in his son and was especially pleased to see that, as he grew up, Edsel seemed to share his interest in machines and technology. Edsel helped out at the factory while still in high school, and afterward, he worked in the family business instead of pursuing college. Father and son had a troubled relationship, however, mostly due to Ford's controlling nature.

Years later, when Edsel died prematurely at age forty-nine from stomach cancer, Ford regretted how he had treated his son, and the memory haunted him for the rest of his life.

Breakthrough

After two years of spending nearly every free minute refining his engine in the small shed behind his home, as well as in a basement room at Edison Illuminating, Ford finally completed his first self-propelled vehicle, which he called the "Quadricycle." On June 4, 1896, Henry Ford drove his Quadricycle out onto the streets of Detroit.

The Quadricycle sat on a steel frame and used a stick instead of a wheel to steer. The seat resembled a toolbox; a rubber belt connected the engine to the rear wire wheels, which looked like they came from a bicycle. Less powerful than a modern lawnmower, the Quadricycle had no brakes and only two forward speeds. But it worked!

Henry Ford (pictured) created a sensation when he drove his Quadricycle on the streets of Detroit for the first time in 1896. It used a doorbell button as its horn.

An Automobile for All

In 1899, Ford decided to leave the Edison Illuminating Company to focus on car building. He later wrote in his autobiography: "I had to choose between my job and my automobile. I chose the automobile."[11] By that time, Henry Ford's ideas about self-propelled vehicles had attracted a good deal of attention. Some wealthy people with money to invest became confident that, with proper support, Ford could turn his horseless carriages into a profitable business. In August 1899, he and some investors formed the Detroit Automobile Company.

Ford and his partners were not alone; other Detroit automakers also saw a bright future in the automobile business and were already selling cars. It soon became clear, however, that Henry Ford and his investors had very different ideas about how to make money in the automobile business.

Different Philosophies

Unlike his competitors, Henry Ford wasn't interested in quickly designing and releasing a car for wealthy people to buy. Instead of bringing a model into production as quickly as possible, Ford kept making changes to his designs. That frustrated his investors, who grew increasingly impatient and angry. In 1901, the investors rebelled, and the Detroit Automobile Company closed.

As Ford and other carmakers struggled to build their new companies at the turn of the century, a small group of daredevil automobile racers had already begun to excite crowds by putting their noisy, smoking, clattering machines to the test on the rough roads that still dominated the American countryside. When the Detroit Automobile Company closed, Ford chose to get involved in racing because "the public thought nothing of a car unless it made speed—unless it beat other racing cars." He hoped that building successful racing cars would make his name, and his cars, well known.[12]

Later in 1901, Ford beat well-known racer and automobile maker Alexander Winton in a two-car race just outside Detroit. A local newspaper reported afterward: "Mr. Ford shot

Henry Ford heavily promoted his automobiles in major media of the time, including newspapers. This 1909 advertisement in the *Saturday Evening Post* promised that consumers could buy essentially the same Model T that had won a coast-to-coast race.

by them as though they were standing still." Over the next few years, Ford built several racing cars, including his famous 999. Unlike his cars before, Ford decided not to drive the 999 during its races. Instead, he hired a driver named Barney Oldfield, and set several new speed records with Oldfield at the wheel. Ford later wrote that "the 999 did what it was intended to do. It advertised the fact that I could build a fast motor car."[13]

Taking Control

Ford's racing success won him the attention and support he was looking for. Partnering with a new group of investors including Alexander Malcomson, Detroit's largest coal dealer, Ford incorporated the Ford Motor Company on June 16, 1903.

Between 1903 and 1908, Ford's company released nine different cars. Each one was named after a letter in the alphabet, and each offered different features and different prices. When Ford insisted on changing the company's approach to focus on simple cars made for the common man, his investors again rebelled. Eventually, he bought out the other shareholders, including Malcomson. They made a healthy profit, but Ford now had the control he wanted.

Henry Ford began to truly realize his vision when he released his Model N. His new model featured many improvements, including the use of stronger and lighter vanadium steel. While its sales climbed impressively, the success of the Model N served only as a precursor for what was to come.

Model T: A Best Seller

Henry Ford had a dream: to build a car that everyone could own and that could handle the rugged roads of the time. Hearkening back to his roots on the farm, Ford believed that this new car had to be cheap, last for many years, and be easy to repair, just like farm equipment. Substance would be more important than style. Ford described his vision this way:

> I will build a motor car for the great multitude. It will be large enough for the family but small enough for the individual to run and care for. It will be constructed of the best materials, by the best men to be hired, after the simplest designs that modern engineering can devise. But it will be so low in price that no man making a good salary will be unable to own one—and enjoy with his family the blessings of hours of pleasure in God's great open spaces.[14]

In October 1908, Ford introduced the Model T, promoting it as a car built for the common man. The Model T was so successful that Ford had to build a new plant in 1910 to keep up with demand. In 1912, he made more than sixty-five thousand Model Ts, a greater number of cars than all other US automakers combined. Model Ts were converted into delivery trucks, taxis, and police cars.[15]

Big Changes

Ford soon realized that, even by hiring more workers and building more factories, he still could not produce enough Model Ts to keep pace with their increasing popularity. In 1913 and 1914, he launched several revolutionary ideas that helped to cement his legacy. These included the moving assembly line, the five-dollar-per-hour wage, and the eight-hour workday. He also purchased farmland along the River Rouge to build a new, more modern factory.

Attempted Peacemaker

As Henry Ford became more successful with his Model T, he tried to use his newfound fame to change people's opinions beyond the automobile business. On November 24, 1915, he called a press conference to announce his plan to end World War I, which had begun the previous year and had embroiled all of Europe in a deadly conflict. A committed pacifist, meaning that he opposed all war, Ford assembled a group of antiwar activists in December of that year, rented an ocean liner named *Oscar II*, and cruised to Europe. Called the "Peace Ship" expedition, Ford planned to arrange meetings with all the warring nations and use the force of his personality to forge an

At its height, Henry Ford's massive River Rouge factory made its own iron, steel, and cement, and employed more than one hundred thousand workers. Today, about six thousand people still work there, and it remains Ford Motor Company's largest single industrial location.

agreement to end the fighting. Thousands of people came to watch the ocean liner leave New York City. Some thought he was crazy. One man sent him two squirrels in a cage. He wrote that they were "to go with the nuts" on board the liner. Sadly, Ford soon realized that no nation would listen to his pleas, and he returned home.[16]

Anti-Semitism

In 1920, Henry Ford did something else that attracted even more attention. In this case, however, the public reacted with disgust, and Henry Ford's reputation would never be the same.

That May, Ford began publishing a controversial series of anti-Semitic articles in his newspaper, the *Dearborn Independent*. They appeared under a bold headline, "The International Jew: The World's Problem." The articles spoke harshly against Jewish Americans; Ford claimed that their control of banks and other industries weakened the country. While Ford stated he did not write the articles himself (although that is debated), they reflected his beliefs, and he approved their publication.

Public backlash came swiftly. Jewish companies and people stopped buying his cars. Famous people, including past presidents, criticized him, and even Ford's wife Clara turned against him. In July 1927, he ceased publishing the newspaper and made a public apology.

End of the T

As America approached the end of the 1920s, the country was evolving in reaction to the growing success of Ford and other automobile manufacturers. More roads had been built and paved, and the strong economy helped people buy more goods and services, including automobiles. The first cars simply provided transportation; new buyers now looked for more choice, comfort, luxury, and style.

The Model T's design had not changed much since it was introduced in 1908, and by the 1920s, sales had begun to plummet. In 1919, Edsel had succeeded his father as president of Ford Motor Company after a stockholder dispute, but his father continued to make all the important decisions. Now many of Ford's executives, including Edsel, believed that the company needed to create fresh models to satisfy the public's new appetites, something Ford's competitors had already done. That did not sit well with Ford, who stubbornly insisted that the Model T should be all that practical buyers should need or want.

It took five years, but continued sales declines as the competition's newer models gained success finally convinced Ford that he needed to replace the Model T. On May 26, 1927, the fifteen-millionth Model T rolled off the Ford assembly line. That same day, Ford announced that the company would begin producing a brand-new vehicle, a redesigned Model A.

The more powerful Model A included new features like windshield wipers and an automatic starter. It proved popular, and sales increased, but the Ford company had already lost its advantage over other automobile manufacturers and would never again regain its position of dominance. Still, sales did grow, until America and the rest of the world fell into a crisis that not even Henry Ford could have predicted.

Economic Collapse

Beginning in 1929, a widespread economic downturn known as the Great Depression forever changed the face of the United States and the rest of the western world. Stocks lost value, banks closed, businesses failed, and jobs vanished. Many people lost their homes, and some even had trouble finding food and shelter for their families.

The depression hurt Detroit more than many other cities because of its dependence on the automobile industry. Total automobile production dropped to half of what it was before World War I, as people could not afford to buy cars. About two in five Detroit workers lost their jobs, and within one year about one-third of all Detroit families had no means of support.[17]

When the depression first started, the stock market's implosion did not affect the Ford Company. Unlike many businesses that sold their stock to the public, Henry Ford and his family owned the company outright, so there was no publicly held stock to collapse. In fact, in 1930, Ford actually made a profit of $40 million. However, that soon changed as fewer people bought cars, and the next year, Ford lost $31 million. By 1932, Ford was forced to lay off nearly half of his workers.

Union Strife

In order to hasten recovery from the depression, President Franklin D. Roosevelt instituted a series of government programs that provided jobs, financial security, and other benefits to Americans suffering at the time. Henry Ford strongly opposed what became known as New Deal policies, especially those that supported the right of workers to form labor unions, groups of employees who band together to demand better wages and working conditions.

In 1935, automobile workers formed their own union, the United Automobile Workers (UAW), but Ford refused to allow his workers to join. He believed that personal success depended on individual effort and self-reliance. He viewed

Henry Ford's reputation suffered when he and his security force leader Harry Bennett violently resisted workers' attempts to unionize. The confrontation is shown here.

government agencies and labor unions the same way he viewed investors, as just another group of people trying to tell him how to run his business.

By 1937, Ford had hired security men to guard the Ford plant. That May, his staff savagely attacked UAW members who were handing out pro-union leaflets at the River Rouge factory. What became known as the Battle of the Overpass was widely reported by newspaper writers and photographers and helped turn the American public against Ford and his harsh treatment of his workers. But, even as the other major car companies decided to make peace with the UAW, Henry Ford still resisted.

Admitting Defeat

Finally, in June 1941, continued pressure from the UAW, the US government, the competition, Edsel, and Clara forced Henry Ford to relent and sign a labor agreement. He was devastated. Longtime Ford production manager Charles Sorensen later wrote that Ford "had been certain that Ford workers would stand by him … He never was the same after that."[18]

Ford was now in his late seventies, and the combination of age and time began to take its toll on his health. He had suffered a stroke in 1938 and, although he recovered, people close to him felt that his memory and mood might have been affected. Ford then suffered another stroke in 1941.

When Edsel died on May 26, 1943, Henry Ford insisted on replacing him as president of the company, even though Clara and Edsel's widow, Eleanor, wanted Edsel's son Henry II to take over. After Ford suffered yet another stroke, Henry II did take over as Ford president in 1945.

An Era Ends

Later that year, an even more severe stroke left Ford mentally and physically weak. Often unable to recognize his family, friends, and old associates, he faded from public view as his family carefully protected his privacy. Then, on April 7, 1947, a blood vessel broke in Henry Ford's brain, and he died at age eighty-three. As always, Clara remained by his side. Two days later, more than one hundred thousand people came to honor him.

After Ford died, the *Detroit News* wrote:

> No other man ever so changed the face of the world in his lifetime as did Henry Ford … He released his countrymen and people everywhere from the older restrictions of locality … To place in the reach of the greatest number of people a useful product which would lift the whole level of living was … a purpose to which he committed a boundless originality and inexhaustible energy.[19]

The country that Henry Ford left behind looked very different than the one of his birth in 1863. Factories had largely replaced farms, and the majority of citizens now lived in cities, linked together by roads filled with automobiles that Ford had built and sold to everyday Americans.

CHAPTER THREE

Predecessors, Partners, and Competitors

Henry Ford had great ideas about how to create and grow the automobile business, but he was far from alone. "There are all kinds of people Henry Ford knows who are all tinkering and playing and trying to produce a prototype," says historian Nancy F. Koehn. "All men, all interested in machines, but all without a big-picture view of what this could become."[1]

Different Kinds

In 1897, bicycle manufacturer Albert Augustus Pope began producing electric cars that ran on batteries but were slow and could only travel short distances. Brothers Francis and Freelan Stanley sold steam-powered cars in

Between 1915 and 1924, Thomas Edison, John Burroughs, Henry Ford, and Harvey Firestone (*left to right*) traveled together, calling themselves the Four Vagabonds.

the very early 1900s, which were fast, but their engines needed time to warm up.

Like Ford, other inventors believed that steam engines were too heavy and unstable, while electric batteries lacked enough power and range. Frank and Charles Duryea built the first American car powered by gas in 1893, and they began selling it three years later. Others quickly joined the chase.

In the introduction to his book *Car Crazy: The Battle for Supremacy Between Ford and Olds and the Dawn of the Automobile Age*, author G. Wayne Miller writes:

> [Ford's] Model T indeed was revolutionary—but it wasn't the first. Oldsmobile founder Ransom Eli Olds built his first car, a three-wheeled thing steered with a tiller and powered by a steam engine, in 1887. The first US vehicle intended for sale was demonstrated in 1893, in Springfield, Massachusetts … Many others in America and Europe, where the auto industry really began, were also building cars—or planning to. Then, between 1900 and 1908, more than five hundred domestic carmakers went into business. Competition was brutal. The vast majority of firms failed.[2]

As he worked to perfect his version of an internal combustion engine, Ford received early crucial support from Thomas Edison, his employer at Edison Illuminating Company.

Friend and Mentor

Born in 1847, Thomas Alva Edison was a major American inventor as well as a leading businessman. He rose from a modest background to introduce major technological breakthroughs

Henry Ford (*left*) learned about electricity while working at Thomas Edison's company in Detroit. Edison (*right*) supported Ford's ideas about building automobiles using internal combustion engines, and the two men later became great friends.

that changed people's lives. His most famous inventions include the incandescent lightbulb, the telegraph, the universal stock ticker (which tracked the changing prices for securities on the stock market), the phonograph (record player), alkaline batteries, and the kinetograph (a camera that produced motion pictures).

Edison always had his eye on the next big thing, and he had already been considering how horseless carriages might change the future of transportation in America. In fact, Edison had tried using batteries to power his own electric vehicles, but he also understood their limitations.

After working at Edison Illuminating for several years, in 1896 Ford received an invitation to attend the company's national convention in New York. Thomas Edison was also there, and when he heard that Ford was working on a car that used internal combustion for its power source, Edison arranged to meet him in person. After Ford explained his ideas and made some sketches on his menu, an intrigued Edison said:

> Young man, that's the thing; you have it. Keep at it. Electric cars must keep near to power stations. The storage battery is too heavy. Steam cars won't do either, for they have to have a boiler and fire. Your car is self-contained—carries its own power plant—no fire, no boiler, no smoke and no steam. You have the thing. Keep at it.[3]

Edison would later praise Ford as a "natural mechanic" and a "natural businessman."

Thomas Edison was forty-nine years old at the time; Ford was thirty-three. Despite the age difference, the two men became close friends for the next three decades, sharing ideas, buying estates near each other, and even vacationing together.

They later joined up with two other influential Americans, businessman Harvey Firestone and poet John Burroughs. Calling themselves the Vagabonds, the four men embarked on two-week camping trips across the United States between 1915 and 1924, often accompanied by US president Warren G. Harding and other leading industrialists.[4]

Always seeking more publicity for himself and his automobiles, Henry Ford made sure that the Vagabonds' exploits were covered by newspapers, magazines, and photographers. Movies of their trips even played in theaters around the United States, leading one observer to write, "The well-equipped excursions were as private and excluded as a Hollywood opening."[5]

Familiar Names

While Edison and others may have appreciated Ford's creativity and passion about building self-powered vehicles, Ford still lacked one important ingredient. He needed money—lots of it—to make his dreams real. Luckily, Ford's ideas helped him attract investors, including wealthy Detroiters like Mayor William C. Maybury and merchants like William H. Murphy (lumber) and Alexander Malcomson (coal). Other automakers also attracted wealthy backers and, like Ford, many of those brands still resonate today.

Born in 1843, Henry Leland was a machinist who made tools for the Union army during the Civil War. He started working with automobiles in 1890 and soon supplied parts to other manufacturers. After Ford left the Henry Ford Company, Leland joined the remaining investors in 1902 to form the Cadillac Automobile Company, building luxury cars named after the French explorer who founded Detroit.

Leland sold Cadillac to General Motors in 1909 but remained an executive until 1917. After that, Leland and his son Wilfred formed another luxury car manufacturer, the Lincoln Motor Company. They named it after President Abraham Lincoln, for whom Leland had actually voted in 1860. The Lincoln Motor Company eventually failed, and Henry Ford bought it, putting son Edsel in charge. Today, the Lincoln brand still exists under the Ford umbrella.

Another Ford contemporary, Ransom E. Olds, manufactured his Oldsmobiles in the nation's first factory devoted solely to car production. Born in Ohio in 1864, one year after Ford, Ransom Olds did not grow up on a farm; he worked in his family's machine and engine shops. Olds built his first gasoline-powered vehicle in 1896, and the following year, he founded Olds Motor Vehicle Company in Lansing, Michigan. Backed by Samuel L. Smith, another rich lumber merchant from the area, Olds moved to Detroit in 1899 and reorganized his business as Olds Motor Works.

In 1901, Olds introduced a small, one-cylinder, "curved-dash" automobile that was light, reliable, and powerful for its time. It gained so much praise that he started full-scale production in 1902. The curved-dash Oldsmobile was the first American car to be produced using the progressive assembly-line system, and Henry Ford adapted similar concepts as he later implemented his own assembly line.

Like Henry Ford, Ransom Olds battled with his investors—he wanted to build smaller cars, while his investors wanted big, expensive vehicles targeted at wealthy buyers. In 1904, Olds left the company he founded to form the Reo Motor Car Company (using his initials, R-E-O.). Ransom's former company struggled after he departed, and in 1908, it merged into what became General Motors.

The Dodge Boys

Former Ford suppliers John and Horace Dodge also grew to be formidable car manufacturers. John Francis Dodge was born in October 1864; his brother Horace Elgin in May 1868. Known to be talented machinists, the Dodge brothers built a successful bicycle business in Detroit before starting their own machine shop.

By 1910, the Dodges ranked among the largest suppliers in Detroit, selling automobile parts to many manufacturers, including Ransom Olds and Henry Ford. Their arrangement with Ford netted them 10 percent of his company's stock.

John and Horace Dodge supplied parts for Henry Ford and other automakers before forming their own car company. Like Ford and other manufacturers from that time, the Dodge company still exists today.

CAR GIANTS REMAIN

The automobile brands that Henry Ford and his competitors founded more than a century ago continue to thrive today. As one of Detroit's "Big Three," Ford Motor Company still manufactures cars under the Ford and Lincoln names. General Motors still operates Buick, Cadillac, and Chevrolet, as well as GMC, while Oldsmobile and Pontiac have vanished.

After big-name company Chrysler joined with German manufacturer Daimler-Benz AG in 1998, it was later sold to outside investors. In 2008, a worldwide recession brought both GM and Chrysler to the brink of failure. The US government under President Barack Obama led both companies through what was then called a "bailout," which included declaring bankruptcy and receiving loans to help them survive. As part of that plan, Chrysler was forced to merge with Italian auto company Fiat. Today, Fiat Chrysler Automobiles includes several brands like Chrysler and Dodge, in addition to Alfa Romeo, Fiat, Jeep, Maserati, and Ram.

Ford had already cut costs prior to the financial crisis and was not part of the 2008 bailout. It did take advantage of government loans to gain access to credit during that time, however, leaving the company in a strong position for the future. Today, Ford continues to increase its investments in new technologies like self-driving and electric cars, as well as services like vehicle-sharing, to make sure it stays strong in the twenty-first century.

However, by 1913, the relationship between Ford and the Dodges had soured. Ford didn't like depending on others for parts; the Dodge brothers knew that he wanted to produce all his own materials. In 1914, they began producing their own cars. Later, they led a stockholder suit against Ford over sharing profits and company control. When the Dodges won their lawsuit, Ford threatened to resign and start another automobile company. His shareholders panicked and sold their stock to Ford and his family. The Dodge brothers eventually sold their Ford stock for $25 million.

By 1920, the Dodge company boasted twenty thousand employees, produced one thousand cars a day, and ranked second behind Ford among all American car manufacturers. Unfortunately, both John and Horace died that year, and in 1925, Dodge heirs sold the company. Walter Chrysler took over management of Dodge three years later.

Combining Assets

William Durant had a different idea about how to structure an automobile company. He had already built other successful businesses in insurance, real estate, and horse-drawn carriages before he got involved in automobile manufacturing in 1886. In 1904, he took over Buick, which was originally founded by Scottish immigrant David Dunbar Buick. By 1908, Durant had built Buick into the nation's leading car company.

Durant actually tried to buy Ford in 1907 but failed. The following year, he founded General Motors, which merged Buick with several other existing automobile manufacturers, including Cadillac, Oldsmobile, and Oakland (later known as Pontiac). By 1910, however, General Motors fell heavily into debt, and Durant lost control of the company.

Durant then joined race-car driver Louis Chevrolet and established Chevrolet Motor Company in 1911. In 1916, he regained control of General Motors and added Chevrolet to his group of companies before being forced out again in 1920.

Legal Assault

Despite competition from other companies, Henry Ford continued to follow his plan of creating one, simple, affordable car that appealed to all Americans. Just as he started to gain momentum, however, several of Ford's competitors banded together and launched a different kind of attack.

More than twenty years earlier, in 1879, lawyer/inventor George Selden had patented the idea for using a gasoline engine to power an automobile. A group of carmakers called the Association of Licensed Automobile Manufacturers (ALAM) now owned the patent. Led by Frederic L. Smith, a hardened executive who had taken over Oldsmobile in 1904, ALAM claimed that anyone selling a car had to pay a licensing fee to the association or face a lawsuit.

Early on, Ford applied to join ALAM but was turned down. He now refused to pay any fees, insisting that gas-powered cars had been created and refined by many different people all over the world rather than by any one inventor.

After a long legal battle that lasted more than eight years, Ford finally won the case and forced ALAM to disband in 1911. The Selden patent case became one of the longest and most expensive lawsuits in the history of American business.[6]

Ford later said that he believed the Selden suit helped increase his company's visibility by casting him as a champion of the common people who challenged a monopoly of luxury automakers: "Probably nothing so well advertised the Ford car and the Ford Motor Company as did this suit. It appeared that we were the underdog and we had the public's sympathy."[7]

Competitors Gain

Henry Ford was a tough competitor, but even people who worked directly with Ford—his partners, coworkers, investors, suppliers, and distributors—held mixed feelings about their relationship with him. While they flocked to Ford's vision, his creativity, and his dedication, they also struggled to deal with his stubbornness, his refusal to consider the ideas of others, and perhaps most of all, his unfailing sense that he and he alone knew what was best for his company and for his fellow Americans.

When automobile customers' tastes began to shift, Ford's executives and members of his own family pleaded with him to replace the Model T with a more modern and attractive car. Ernest Kanzler, Edsel's brother-in-law, also worked at Ford. Knowing how difficult it was to confront Ford in person, Kanzler wrote him a letter in 1926 that summarized both the need for change as well as the difficulty in dealing with Ford's personality:

> I can write certain things that I find it difficult to say to you. It is one of the handicaps of the power of your personality which perhaps you least of all realize, but most people when with you hesitate to say what they think … We have not gone ahead in the last few years …whereas competition has made great strides. You have always said you either go forwards or backwards, you can't stand still.[8]

Alfred P. Sloan became president and chief executive of General Motors in 1923. He reorganized the company into five separate automotive brands, offering consumers a choice of style and cost.

Ford did not accept the criticism well; he remained steadfast in his opposition and even drove Kanzler away from the company. Describing that time, historian Nancy F. Koehn noted that: "[Ford] was so maniacally committed to his vision.

The same thing that makes him successful now begins to create more vulnerability for him."[9]

Rivals such as General Motors president Alfred P. Sloan were quick to take advantage, and they began to adjust their approach to satisfy new consumer appetites. In their book *In Their Time: The Greatest Business Leaders of the Twentieth Century*, authors Anthony J. Mayo and Nitin Nohria describe GM's new direction:

> Taking the helm of General Motors Corporation in 1923, Alfred P. Sloan Jr. revolutionized the growing automobile business by giving consumers a choice of color, size and style. He understood the underlying current in America at the time, a current that longed for individuality, freedom and status. Instead of one car for all people, Sloan's General Motors produced a suite of cars, each aimed at a particular social status. Beyond freedom of choice, Sloan also gave consumers "freedom of purchase" by offering cars on installment plans. He gave the consumers the illusion that they could have it all, a higher-priced, uniquely designed car on credit. By 1927, one-third of all cars were purchased on credit.[10]

Ford's slow response to problems with the Model T allowed his rivals to establish themselves in both the United States market and abroad. Ford remained a major force, but his days of total dominance had ended, and Ford's company now faced real and permanent competition for mass car production.

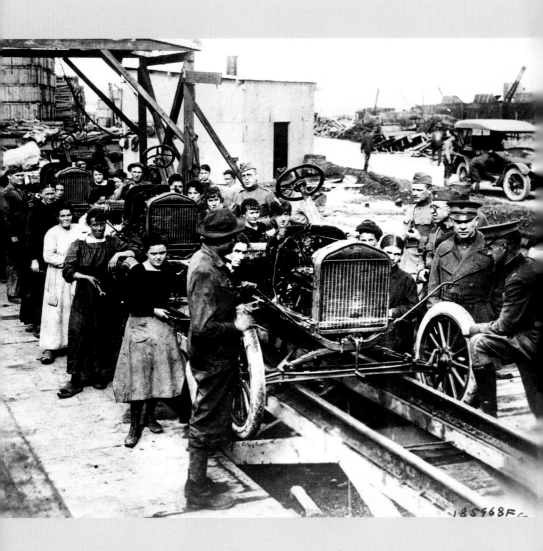

CHAPTER FOUR

Historical Accomplishments

H istorians credit Henry Ford with a long list of achievements—so many, in fact, that it's difficult to adequately credit them all, much less choose one or two as ranking higher in importance than others. Fifteen million Model Ts? The assembly line? The $5 hourly wage? The eight-hour workday? Those and other feats continue to reinforce Henry Ford's reputation today.

All of the Above

Although each accomplishment carries its own weight, the true secret to Henry Ford's success lies in his uncanny ability to view each idea as simply one component in a greater plan to transport everyday Americans away from

Henry Ford's assembly line included women and paved the way for mass production of automobiles.

their isolation, their inefficiency, and their horses and into the modern industrial world. Taken as a whole, Ford and his practices managed to change the way that Americans viewed work, consumption, and leisure.

You will often hear people say that Ford "invented" the assembly line, or standardized parts, or even the automobile itself. In truth, those ideas existed years before Ford applied them to his own business. However, he had a great ability to envision what more could be done with processes that others may have already thought of.

In turn, many of his ideas have been broadly applied to areas beyond the automotive business. Ford himself held more than fifty patents for designing auto parts and systems alone, including such diverse areas as transmissions, steering, suspension, cooling, and engines.

Different Way of Thinking

Henry Ford was by no means the first person to view automobiles as a great business opportunity. However, he did see the business very differently than his peers. Most car manufacturers at that time believed in several principles: separate models should be produced for buyers with different needs, that cars should be built only after buyers had already placed an order, and that wealthy buyers provided the most likely customers and the most profit per car.

Ford believed that success required thinking about car manufacturing as being no different than any other business:

> The way to make automobiles is to make one automobile like another automobile, to make them all alike, to make them come through the factory

just alike; just like one pin is like another pin when it comes from a pin factory, or one match is like another match when it comes from a match factory.[1]

Ford wanted to build cars first, and then wait for customers to buy them in the same way they bought other merchandise from stores. In his book *Henry Ford: Auto Tycoon*, Michael Pollard describes how Ford viewed the business:

> By 1903, [Ford's] ideas were clearly formed. The industry would lure customers into showrooms rather than wait for them to call. It would offer them cars they could drive away then and there. It would make the ownership of a car so attractive, even essential, that every family would want one. By building cars in large numbers, it would be possible to bring down the price.[2]

In order to do that, Ford had to produce cars more quickly and cheaply than other makers. One of his first decisions was to use parts made by outside companies, which Ford's workers could then fashion into a finished product. According to author Ronald Reis, in 1903 the Ford Motor Company was strictly an assembly operation:

> No car parts were actually manufactured by Ford. Engines, transmissions and axles, for example, came from the Dodge Brothers Machine Shop. The new company obtained its wooden bodies and cushions from the C. R. Wilson Carriage Company. The Prudden Company built the Model A's wheels. And the Hartford Rubber Works Company provided tires.[3]

As sales grew, Ford became increasingly focused on how to make his factories more productive with less waste. During his early days working at the Flower Brothers Machine Shop in Detroit, Ford became frustrated with what he saw as an inefficient workflow. Men constantly shifted from one job to another; workers were told in the middle of a task to stop what they were doing to move to another project, or sent to a different area to retrieve a tool or part.

Even Ford's first cars were built by separate teams of mechanics who worked on four cars at a time, continuously circling the car as they worked, and ordering parts from the warehouse as they needed them. Each stage had to be completed before moving to the next, and lack of coordination led to mistakes and poor quality.

The Assembly Line

Ford hated wasting time, so he took steps to increase efficiency at his shop. He hired advisors to examine all of his business processes to determine what could be changed or improved. One expert looked at Ford's operations and suggested that each man specialize in one or two tasks rather than switching from one to the other. Another advisor helped plan and build the assembly line by dividing tasks into many small, separate steps.

Ford himself visited plants in other industries to see how they operated. At a meatpacking plant, he noted how products moved along a conveyor belt. At a sewing machine factory, Ford witnessed how each worker put together only one piece of a sewing machine.[4]

Late in 1913, all of Henry Ford's efforts to improve efficiency came to fruition. That fall, he introduced the world's first, moving, automobile assembly line at his Highland Park factory.

In her book *Henry Ford: The Car Man*, author Carin T. Ford describes how it worked: "Pieces of the car traveled along a moving belt. As the car parts rolled by, each worker stood in one place doing the same job over and over. One worker might fasten a bolt or tighten a nut, but he did not do both of these jobs."[5]

Henry Ford also described the idea behind his assembly line: "We began taking the work to the men instead of the men to the work." After seeing it in action, a reporter for one newspaper called it an "industrial marvel."[6]

Goals Achieved

Henry Ford's assembly line generated impressive results. In 1913, the company produced just over 168,000 Model Ts. In 1914, the first full year for the assembly line, production increased to more than 248,000. Under the old system, it took about twelve hours to build a car. The assembly line reduced that to about ninety minutes.

The introduction of the assembly line also provided Ford with an additional benefit. Since each task was repetitive, managers could observe and measure how long it took to finish each step. That information helped Ford and his managers to better plan their production and delivery schedules and to build more accurate budgets and forecasting tools.

Controlling All Elements

By the end of 1913, Ford's sales increased to the point that about one of every two cars sold in the United States was a Ford. As his sales grew, however, Ford ran into another problem. The heavy demand put pressure on his suppliers to increase their volume as well, and they began to experience problems building enough parts and maintaining their own quality. In response, Ford decided to expand his capacity to build and supply his own parts. Author Michael Pollard writes: "The Ford Company became what is known in today's management language as a vertically integrated business, in which as many manufacturing processes as possible were carried out under direct company control."[7]

Unexpected Consequences

Ford's introduction of the assembly line certainly improved the company's production, efficiency, and profitability, but something also happened that Ford did not expect: workers hated it.

The sudden transition from building complete cars to working on an assembly line shook many employees to their core. In that era, autoworkers considered themselves to be skilled craftspeople; they had been trained to use their hands to perform expert tasks. Teams worked together to build finished products, including cars. They took pride in completing a project and in working as a team.

On an assembly line, however, workers performed one, repetitive task, over and over again. No particular skill was necessary; employees now felt that, like parts in a machine, they too were interchangeable and easily replaced. They no longer felt connected, either to their coworkers or to the finished product.

Assembly-line workers also had to work much faster than before and make no mistakes. As the assembly line moved faster, workers had to keep pace. In just a short period of time, workers on the line began to feel like their lives had no meaning.

When Henry Ford and his investors formed the Ford Motor Company, he owned stock just like his partners. This certificate shows his official stock holdings for the company.

Employee reaction turned out to be swift and decisive. Many workers could not handle the new working environment and quit after just a few days. Soon the problems multiplied, and the company began to lose between 40 and 60 percent of its workforce every month. When Ford gave a Christmas bonus to workers who had been there at least three years, only 640 out of 15,000 employees qualified. Company managers calculated that, in order to keep 100 employees for more than a few days, they needed to hire more than 1,000 to account for turnover.

Constantly hiring and training new workers was inefficient and expensive for Henry Ford, so he quickly devised a solution that not only shocked the United States auto industry but made headlines around the world.

Five Dollars a Day

Early in 1914, Henry Ford announced that his company intended to double the average worker's daily wage from less than $2.40 to $5 per hour. Rather than simply call it a wage hike, Ford positioned the move as a desire to share company profits with his workers. He also felt that higher salaries would pay off for his company in the long run. In his book *Masters of Enterprise: Giants of American Business from John Jacob Astor and J. P. Morgan to Bill Gates and Oprah Winfrey*, author, educator, and historian Henry W. Brands describes Ford's reasoning in this way:

> Calling his new system a "prosperity-sharing plan," Ford envisioned the benefits of higher wages rippling onward through the economy as a whole … Ford explained that "Our own sales depend in a measure upon the wages we pay. If we can distribute high wages, then that money is going to be spent and it will serve to make storekeepers and distributors and manufacturers and workers in other lines more prosperous and their prosperity will be reflected in our sales."[8]

When the news got out, newspapers all around the country heralded the story, and magazines wrote in-depth features on Ford's life. On January 11, 1914, the *New York Times* proclaimed that "[Ford] shocks businesses by agreeing to share profits with workers." Another newspaper described it as "a magnificent act of generosity."[9]

Not everyone agreed with Ford's approach, however. One newspaper declared that Ford had committed "economic blunders, if not crimes" that would hurt all of America. Many of Ford's competitors also attacked the wage increase, with one calling it "the most foolish thing ever attempted in the industrial world."[10]

Ford relished the publicity he and his company received after announcing the wage hike. More importantly, he proved his critics wrong. Thousands of excited workers responded almost immediately to the promise of significantly higher pay and flocked to find jobs at the Ford factory. Robert Casey, an automotive historian and a former curator at the Henry Ford Museum, said that it was the "same work, just as boring, just as repetitive, just as hard. But, you got people who never dreamed that they could make this much money."[11]

In addition to the pay increase, Ford also shortened the workday from nine hours to eight. While he felt that the shorter day would help workers to be more productive, the move also allowed him to operate his factory twenty-four hours a day by moving to three eight-hour shifts.

The combination of higher pay and shorter shifts produced the result Ford was looking for. The number of absent workers declined from 10 percent a day to less than 0.5 percent. In 1913, Ford hired fifty-three thousand replacement workers; in 1915, the number dropped to two thousand. Henry Ford believed he actually saved money and made more profit by raising workers' wages; workers were more productive, and Ford spent less on turnover and absenteeism. Plus, he claimed another benefit: workers now had more money to buy products, including Ford cars.

The Model T

The assembly line, the $5 hourly wage, and the eight-hour workday transformed attitudes about work and productivity. When it came to capturing the public's imagination, however, perhaps nothing could eclipse the culmination of Henry's original dream: building a car for the masses.

In September 1908, newspapers and magazines announced the arrival of an exciting, revolutionary automobile. This newcomer, the advertisement said, was "powerful, speedy and enduring—a car that looks good and is as good as it looks. Better features or as high-grade materials cannot be found in any other car at any price. A better car is not and cannot be made." The new model, the advertisement continued, was to be sold for $850. This was "several hundred dollars less than the lowest of the rest."[12] The car was Ford's Model T. It was not

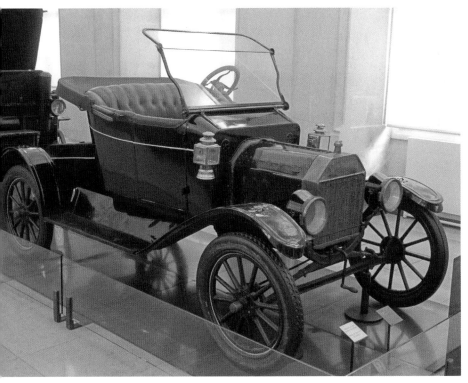

This Ford Model T was built in 1908, the first year of production. Hailed as the first car designed for everyday Americans, more than fifteen million Model Ts were built before Ford discontinued the model in 1927.

FORD'S DREAM CAR

Still one of the best-selling cars in US history, Ford's Model T could turn in a 12-foot (3.7-meter) circle, travel rough and rocky roads, and pull itself out of loose sand. It was very fast by the standards of the time. Its top speed was 45 miles (72 kilometers) per hour. It delivered 25 miles per gallon (10.6 km per liter) at what was then 20 cents per gallon (just over 5 cents per liter).

People soon began to refer to the car as the "tin Lizzie," with Lizzie being common slang for a good and dependable servant. One historian compared the public's appetite for Model Ts to a huge vacuum cleaner sitting at the Ford plant's entrance, sucking each car out with a loud "whoosh" as soon as it rolled off the assembly line. By the end of the 1920s, Ford had sold more than fifteen million Model Ts.[14]

designed to be stylish or powerful. Ford believed that people wanted a "no-frills mechanical workhorse for everyday use."[13]

The Model T used a new kind of steel that was lighter, stronger, and more resistant to rust. It rode higher to handle rough roads and cart paths. It also placed the steering wheel on the left side of the car, where it remains today in America and much of the world.

Earlier cars often mounted their steering wheels on the right so drivers could see ruts and the edge of the road on their side. Ford, however, anticipated that more and improved roads would lead to heavier traffic, and that drivers would be better served by sitting on the left so that they could see cars approaching from the opposite direction.

It's difficult to understand today how much impact the Model T made on the lives of everyday Americans. "The Model T changed everything," says historian Greg Grandin. "It gave people a new sense of power and authority and control over their lives. You could go wherever you wanted and you could go by yourself." Thousands of people wrote letters to Ford, thanking him for the Model T. A farm wife from Rome, Georgia, wrote, "Your car lifted us out of the mud. It brought joy into our lives." By 1923–1924, two-thirds of all the automobiles registered in the United States were Model Ts.[15]

Creative Approaches

As Henry Ford continued to look for better and more efficient ways to operate his company, he wasn't afraid to challenge established norms in arenas beyond automobile manufacturing. In 1920, he bought the Detroit, Toledo, and Ironton (DT&I) Railroad. The DT&I linked Detroit with coal and iron mines to the South and intersected with fifteen other railroad lines. Ford wanted to use the railroad to move raw materials to his factories and then transport finished cars to other cities, boat terminals, and customers around the United States and the world. To make shipping even more efficient, he also began to build factories in other cities, then shipped parts to be assembled and sold in those locations.

More Opportunities

Henry Ford is also known for establishing perhaps the most diverse workforce for his time. He hired African Americans during a period when much of America practiced racial discrimination, and he hired immigrants and those with physical challenges. In 1930, one out of four Ford employees had some kind of physical handicap, and at one point, more than 7 percent of Ford workers were foreign born, representing fifty-eight different nationalities and speaking more than seventy languages and dialects. Ford gave them jobs and helped improve their education, health, and living conditions.[16]

He also hired more women and paid them higher wages than other companies, but there was a catch. Ford still believed that a woman's traditional place was in the home, so many women he hired had to prove that they were the "the sole support of some next of kin."

Ford also established other conditions that employees had to follow. He created a sociological department that visited employees' homes and enforced Ford's personal standards of behavior, including no alcohol or smoking, and saving money for their families. His workers usually tolerated this invasion into their private lives in exchange for Ford's higher wages and a safe place to work. Historian Steven Watts says that Ford "came to believe that he was not only an economic entrepreneur but a prophet of proper living."[17]

"We want to make men in this factory as well as automobiles," Ford once said.[18] However, for him, there was always one, main goal: to build cars, as many and as efficiently as possible.

CHAPTER FIVE

Shaped By His Era

Henry Ford lived during an incredible period of change in America. Born in the middle of the most destructive war that the country has ever known, he grew up watching his rural, agricultural world slowly fade into the past as new technological developments sparked his imagination. After moving to Detroit, he glimpsed firsthand how new machines could alter the lives of ordinary Americans and offer a much better life than would have been possible just a few years earlier. The world as Ford knew it would never be the same. Rather than sit back and wait for the changes that would be in store, he decided he would take charge and help lead the way.

Throughout his life, Henry Ford enjoyed "getting his hands dirty" by personally working on his automobiles.

Early Discipline

Ford hated the daily tedium and wasted time of farm life. He later wrote in his autobiography *My Life and Work* that, "Even when I was very young I suspected that much might somehow be done in a better way. That is what took me into mechanics— although my mother always said that I was a born mechanic."[1]

Ford credited his mother with teaching him important values that stayed with him throughout his life. Mary Ford "believed in doing chores well, with little wasted effort," he recalled. "She was ... orderly and thorough, and she demanded that from us."[2]

Later in life, Ford spoke to a reporter about his mother's influence:

> She taught me that disagreeable jobs call for courage and patience, and self-discipline, and she also taught me that "I don't want to" gets a fellow nowhere ... My mother used to say, when I grumbled about it, "Life will give you many unpleasant tasks to do; your duty will be hard and disagreeable and painful to you at times, but you must do it. You may have pity on others, but you must not pity yourself. Do what you find to do, and what you know you must do, to the best of your ability.[3]

Mary Ford possessed another quality that her son valued—a selfless devotion to her family and a commitment to do what she thought was best, even if her family disagreed. "[She was] of that rarest type," Ford said after his mother died, "one who so loved her children that she did not care whether they loved her. What I mean by this is that she would do whatever she considered necessary for our welfare, even if she thereby lost our good will."[4]

Ford seems to have followed his mother's example as he married, had a son, and founded his businesses. He believed he knew what people needed and how they should behave, even if it turned his family, investors, workers, and customers against him. Some of his decisions permanently damaged his relationships with others, especially with his financial backers and his own son.

Henry Ford was only twelve when his mother Mary died at the age of thirty-five. This is a depiction of her at age twenty-seven or twenty-eight.

Self-Reliance

Ford also took to heart his mother's respect for self-reliance and hard work and applied it to his own life. He later wrote in his autobiography:

> Every advance begins in a small way and with the individual. The mass can be no better than the sum of the individuals. Advancement begins with the man himself; when he advances from self-interest to strength of purpose; when he advances from hesitancy to decisive directness; when he advances from immaturity to maturity of judgment ... why, then the world advances. The advance is not easy. We live in flabby times when men are being taught that everything ought to be easy. Work that amounts to anything will never be easy.[5]

Ford always fully committed himself to any task, and he looked for those same qualities in the people he worked with. Douglas Brinkley, a professor of history at Rice University, has said that Ford "promoted people who had a drive, people that didn't sleep, people that wanted to work harder [and] really wanted to perfect his company."[6]

Down in the Trenches

When he'd start a new project, Ford would sometimes close off a secret room where he and a handpicked group of engineers, mechanics, and designers could work in secret. Ford thought nothing of getting down on the floor and working alongside his team, and they loved him for it. One of his mechanics recalled: "He went out with us many a time. Mr. Ford would not let anything go out of the shop unless he was satisfied that it was nearly as perfect as you could make it. He wanted it right."[7]

Greg Grandin, a professor of history and the author of *Fordlandia: The Rise and Fall of Henry Ford's Forgotten Jungle City*, believes that Ford's hands-on attitude helped to increase his appeal, once saying that "I think that the mechanical intuition that he had created a kind of charisma that drew people to him." Ford's enthusiasm and focus helped convince others that they were working on something important. "Even if you were on the floor assembling these cars, you knew that you were part of something that was happening, something new, something that was changing the company," says former Henry Ford Museum curator Robert Casey.[8]

Ford's hard life on the farm also taught him not to waste resources and to try to use farm products in his own factories. He used wheat gluten to manufacture some components on his Model T, and soybean oil in paint and for fluids used in shock absorbers. Soybean fiber and waste material was included in products that ranged from horn buttons and window strips to car seat fabric.

Mistrust of Wealth

Sketching out ideas, recruiting team members, and building cars came easily to Ford. Running a business, however, turned out to be much more difficult. Ford had no real experience in designing projects, setting budgets, or managing employees. Farm life had taught him to rely on himself rather than on other people, so he now found it difficult to accept criticism or take advice.

Ford also came from moderate means, and he mistrusted anyone with wealth. His determination to produce a car for the masses and do things his own way often put him at odds with his financial backers, who expected their opinions to be considered before he made decisions and also hoped for quick profits from their investments. For his part, Ford referred to stockholders who wanted big rewards for small investments as "parasites."[9]

Historian Douglas Brinkley states that Ford "hated the people who invested in him. Loathed them ... [Ford believed that] these are the people that looked down on the slang of the farm and the kinfolk of his that had worked the land for generations. He did not like these people."[10]

Ford's conflicts with investors caused him to leave several companies, but he quickly recovered. "Even after all the failures that Henry Ford had," says historian and author Steven Watts, "he was convinced that he should plunge ahead. He wasn't convinced that he had failed. It was some sort of momentary setback. It's an absolute confidence in your own talent ... and your own vision of doing something important."[11]

Public Hero

Ford's supreme confidence served him well as he pursued his dream of building a car for everyone, and his tremendous success with the Model T ultimately proved him right. Not only did the Model T outsell all its competitors combined and rank as the most-purchased automobile of its time, it also served to establish Henry Ford's reputation as a national personality and a hero of the common man.

In truth, Henry Ford craved publicity. He enjoyed granting interviews, he often invited reporters to come on vacations with his friends, and he was delighted that people wanted to hear his opinions on any and all subjects. In his book *The Ford Century: Ford Motor Company and the Innovations that Shaped the World*, author Russ Banham writes that, "Henry's rural background, wholesome habits and love of nature had endeared him to many Americans, and his unabashed opinions were good copy for the journalists who shadowed his every move."[12]

Opinion Turns

In the summer of 1919, however, Henry Ford got a taste of how quickly his reputation could tarnish.

Three years earlier, President Woodrow Wilson had sent troops to the US-Mexico border due to tension between the two countries. Henry Ford opposed the move, and the *Chicago Tribune* labeled him an "ignorant idealist … and an anarchist enemy of the nation." Ford sued the paper for libel. When the case finally came to trial, newspapers across the country covered Ford's every word as he took the stand to testify. Over eight days of pointed questioning, Ford's lack of formal schooling became evident. The *Tribune*'s lawyers portrayed Ford as terribly ill-informed and woefully ignorant of subjects like world history. Many newspapers now described the legendary creator of the Model T as nothing more than an inarticulate "rural rube" who had just been lucky in his business. The *New York Times* wrote: "Mr. Ford has been submitted to a severe examination of his intellectual qualities. He has not received a pass." Another paper, the *New York Post*, exclaimed that "the man is a joke." Although Ford won his legal case, he bitterly resented the coverage he received.[13]

Still Popular

After the trial, however, tens of thousands of people, many of them from the same rural areas where Ford was born, sent him letters of support. They thought that the *Tribune*'s lawyers took advantage of Ford and that he had been misrepresented by the press and city society. The *Journal*, a small newspaper in Fairbury, Nebraska, rose to Ford's defense, writing, "A few less smart-aleck attorneys and a few more Henry Fords, and the world would have less troubles and more to eat." For those people and many others, Ford had become an even more popular folk hero than before the trial.[14]

Problems with Prejudice

Many historians believe that Ford's anti-Semitic publications arose at least in part due to his antagonism toward people with money. Beginning in 1920, Ford's newspaper, the *Dearborn Independent,* published the first of ninety-one consecutive articles that accused Jews of controlling financial systems around the world. The paper was distributed through Ford dealerships across the United States, and the articles were also compiled into a series of books that were published in sixteen languages.

Whether Ford wrote the articles himself or just approved them being published remains unclear, as do the reasons why he chose to take such a public stand against Jews. We do know that he did not trust bankers or wealthy investors, and perhaps those views extended to wealthy and influential people within the Jewish community.

Regardless of his reasons, his positions sparked a severe backlash. Former presidents Woodrow Wilson and William

Howard Taft spoke out against Ford and his anti-Semitic remarks, and members of his own family criticized him, including his wife Clara. To some people, Ford's comments "reflected his lack of education. He had never trusted well-educated people—he preferred the simple farmers and mechanics he had grown up with."[15]

Despite heavy criticism, Ford stubbornly kept at it until Jewish lawyer and farm cooperative leader Aaron Shapiro sued him for libel and forced a settlement. In July 1927, Ford made a public apology and discontinued publishing the *Dearborn Independent*.

Self-Promotion

Despite the damage that his anti-Semitism caused to his reputation, Ford continued to seek publicity for himself and his company, taking increasingly stronger steps to shape and control his own message. He advertised heavily in newspapers, magazines, and another new technology—radio. Ford also assembled a powerful network of local dealers, small businessmen who built showrooms in towns across the United States to exclusively promote and sell Ford products. Ford even established his own film house to make movies about the Ford company, as well as himself.

As he carefully continued to build up his image as a genius inventor with simple tastes and a disdain for riches, some experts think that he started to believe his own headlines and that his ego grew ever stronger. It all came to a head when Ford battled his advisors and even his family over his most prized accomplishment—his Model T.

Over the years, Henry Ford made many statements about how businesses needed to keep moving forward to avoid

CONFLICTED
RELATIONSHIP

When Edsel Ford became the Ford Company's president, he tried to convince his father that the auto business was changing and that they needed to develop new models.

Perhaps nothing better demonstrates Henry Ford's singular focus on doing things his way than his treatment of his only child, Edsel.

When Edsel was twenty-six years old, Ford installed his son as president of Ford Motor Company. Unlike his father, Edsel believed that automobiles could be stylish and comfortable as well as functional. In 1922, he encouraged his father to purchase the Lincoln Motor Company and position the brand as a luxury alternative to Ford.

Although Edsel was now president of Ford, his father still made the big decisions and often contradicted Edsel's policies. Senior Ford managers quickly learned that it served their best interest to listen to Mr. Ford rather than to his son.

While some historians think that Henry Ford intended to toughen Edsel up and teach him to be a better leader, others believe that he simply thought that he and he alone knew what was best for his company. Charles Sorensen, a high-ranking executive at the Ford company, once said, "Henry Ford's greatest achievement was changing the face of America and putting the world on wheels. His greatest failure was his treatment of his only son, Edsel."[16]

failure. "The only real mistake is the one from which we learn nothing," he once said. On another occasion, he stated, "Businesses that grow by development and improvement do not die."[17]

Unfortunately, Henry Ford sometimes had trouble following his own advice, never more clearly than when Model T sales began to sag. Ford could not understand how people could now choose luxury, comfort, and style over the dependable and practical Model T that he had designed specifically for them. His failure to react to changing times ultimately allowed his competitors to topple the Ford company from its once-dominant perch high above the automotive industry.

Longing for the Past

In 1916, Ford told the *Chicago Tribune* that, "History is more or less bunk." However, Ford did not intend to devalue the importance of history itself. He really meant that people usually study the accomplishments of famous and influential leaders but do not learn about the lives of ordinary people. As he grew older and saw the world changing around him, Ford gained an even greater appreciation of his past and yearned to return to the simpler days of his youth. Referring to his statement three years earlier, in 1919 he declared that American history was "the only history that is worth observing" and that "We're going to build a museum that's going to show industrial history, and it won't be bunk."[18]

In 1929, Ford opened the Edison Institute, now called the Henry Ford, a library and museum located in Dearborn, Michigan. In 1933, he expanded his tribute to the past when he established Greenfield Village, a collection of historic

Henry Ford built Greenfield Village to show how America had changed and to portray a way of life that he felt was slipping away.

buildings on 200 acres (80 hectares) next to the Edison Institute. The village quickly grew to include hundreds of historic buildings and artifacts that Ford bought, then carefully took apart, transported, and rebuilt. Ford wanted to recreate a rural town to commemorate America's past.

In his later years, Ford spent more time on his farm and in Greenfield Village than in his factories. Historian Steven Watts says that Greenfield Village "becomes a monument not only to the American past, but to [Ford's] past as well. He seemed to be yearning to somehow recapture the kind of society and culture that the automobile and the [building of the] River Rouge [factory] had essentially destroyed."

Professor and author Greg Grandin adds, "You have him raising River Rouge, which is this enormous cathedral to industry. And in the shadows of the River Rouge he's building this nineteenth-century testament to a receding America."[19]

Today, Greenfield Village still exists. It includes homes and workplaces of Ford and other famous Americans, as well as buildings such as Thomas Edison's New Jersey laboratory and a courthouse where Abraham Lincoln practiced law. The site also boasts a steam-powered paddleboat and several locomotives, as well as English and early American homes, public buildings, and craft shops.

In many ways, Henry Ford serves as an example of his age. He relentlessly pursued a new and better future, yet he still held fast to values that hearkened back to his childhood years spent on the farm. He changed the world for everyone, yet he wound up resisting the very forces of change that he helped to create.

CHAPTER SIX

Driving New Directions

W hen Henry Ford passed the leadership of Ford Motors to his grandson in 1945, Henry II assumed control of one of the largest companies in the world. It had more than 120,000 workers and was worth more than $1 billion, nearly $14 billion in today's dollars.

More Than Riches

According to *Forbes* magazine, at the time of his death, Ford had a net worth of nearly $2 billion measured in today's dollars. Original investors in Ford Motor Company also enjoyed huge windfalls. James Couzens helped build Ford's company and originally invested $900; when the

The iconic Ford Mustang first appeared in 1965 and remains a strong seller more than fifty years later. This version appeared in 2012.

Ford family finally bought back his stock in 1919, its value had soared to more than $29 million.[1]

However, Henry Ford's real story isn't about wealth. It's true that he did not actually invent the automobile, the internal combustion engine, or the assembly line. In many ways, however, his accomplishment was far greater. Ford incorporated, adapted, and improved his ideas and those of others to accomplish his goal of making cars for everyone, a radically different vision that few people shared at the time. He also understood how concepts like higher wages and shorter workdays could not only improve people's lives but also help Ford to sell more cars.

Changed the World

Lee Iacocca, former head of both Ford Motor Company and Chrysler, once worked as a trainee in the Ford River Rouge Plant near Detroit. In his introduction for Don Mitchell's book *Driven: A Photobiography of Henry Ford*, Iacocca writes:

> The boss [Ford] was a genius, and his mark on history is extraordinary … He thought that guys who made cars ought to be able to afford one themselves. He figured that if he paid his factory workers a real living wage and produced more cars in less time for less money, everyone would buy them. And they did.

Iacocca further explains, however, that Ford's lasting influence extends well beyond cars, wages, and living conditions:

> Ford was smart enough to know that making a car wasn't enough. Just like horses, cars need to be fed, so he pushed for gas stations to be built everywhere.

He established a dealer-franchise system to sell and service cars, and his campaign for better roads led to an interstate highway system that is still the envy of the world.[2]

Changing the Landscape

When Ford died in 1947, a Detroit newspaper wrote, "Ford established a new age—it might also be said a new civilization." His mass marketing of automobiles certainly helped change the American countryside. In 1909, America only had about 700 miles (1227 km) of paved highways. By 1930, the figure skyrocketed to 100,000 miles (160,934 km). People now traveled more often and for longer distances. Affordable cars and better roads also allowed workers to live miles away from their jobs, and suburbs began to rise up from the rural farmland outside of big cities. Planners built new communities with cars in mind.[3]

Other businesses now grew to support automobiles. In addition to gas stations and repair shops, restaurants appeared on roadsides, along with drive-through lanes and parking lot services. National parks and seaside resorts attracted new throngs of visitors, which led to more hotels and motels. The rubber industry grew as the need for tires exploded.

Some Negatives

Not all the effects were positive, however. Before automobiles replaced horses, city streets had been choked with piles of manure and the smell of urine. The automobile changed all that, but not always for the better. Exhaust fumes and noisy engines replaced the sounds and smells of horses, while accidents and injuries increased as these new machines competed with old-fashioned carriages and pedestrians for dominance on city streets and even rural roads.

People and Machines

Continuing the effects of the Industrial Revolution, the mass production of automobiles further accelerated the shift from an agrarian to an industrial economy, introducing both advantages and disadvantages. While Ford's ideas like raising pay and shortening the workday helped to improve personal wealth, productivity, and working conditions, many also believe that the assembly line and other methods of mass production tended to "dehumanize" the workplace, as speed and efficiency took precedence over skill and personal satisfaction.

In his 1936 landmark film *Modern Times*, silent film star Charlie Chaplin included a scene where his character works on a factory assembly line. In an essay he adapted from his book, *Chaplin: Genius of the Cinema*, author Jeffrey Vance describes both why Chaplin filmed the scene and why it still applies today:

> Chaplin was struck with the idea for the film after learning about healthy young men who had been lured away from their farms to work in factories in Detroit but, after several years on the assembly line, succumbed to nervous breakdowns. "Modern Times" evolved into a comedy that embraces difficult subjects such as … the tyranny of automation … [and] the struggle to eschew alienation and preserve humanity in a modern, mechanized world.[4]

In his movie *Modern Times*, British comedian and director Charlie Chaplin (*right*) showed how difficult it was to work on a factory assembly line and perform repetitive tasks.

Henry Ford's many accomplishments attracted recognition and awards both during his life and after his death. In 1928, he received the Franklin Institute's Elliott Cresson Medal, and in 1946, he was inducted into the Automotive Hall of Fame. The United States Postal Service later honored Ford with a postage stamp and, in 1999, a Gallup poll included Henry in their list of Widely Admired People of the Twentieth Century. However, in 1938, Ford was also awarded Nazi Germany's

Grand Cross of the German Eagle, and people accused him of being sympathetic to Nazism and their anti-Semitic policies.

The Deuce Takes Control

Henry Ford's legacy continued after his death. His grandson, Henry Ford II, was only twenty-eight years old when he succeeded his grandfather as Ford president in 1945. Sometimes referred to as "Hank the Deuce" or "HF2," Ford II inherited a company that was struggling.

World War II had just ended, and most factories in the United States and abroad had only begun to transition away from war production; many in Europe had been damaged or destroyed during the long years of conflict. Raw materials were in short supply, and research and development for consumer products had lagged. Ford still had its loyal consumer base and reputation, however, and Henry II immediately got to work.

As an important first step, the inexperienced Henry II brought in a team of outside experts to help streamline and restructure the company. They questioned old ways of doing things and designed new and innovative products. Henry II also sold Ford stock to the public for the first time and later established a new world headquarters in Dearborn, Michigan, in 1956.

Public Works

While he was alive, Henry Ford steered significant amounts of his vast fortune toward helping those in need. Following his motto, "Help the other fellow," Ford assisted many medical facilities and donated millions to build and support the Henry Ford Hospital, which opened in 1915. He also started the

After replacing his grandfather as president of Ford in 1945, Henry Ford II restructured the company to effectively compete in the post–World War II era. He also expanded its role in supporting charitable, educational, and community causes.

Henry Ford Trade School next to his factory in Highland Park, teaching drafting, welding, and mechanics to local boys, and created the Edison Institute school system, which allowed students to attend from kindergarten through high school with no tuition.[5]

After taking over the company, Henry Ford II continued and even expanded his grandfather's efforts. In 1936, Ford senior had established the Ford Foundation to "receive and administer funds for scientific, educational and charitable purposes, all for the public welfare and for no other purpose." Ford II continued that work and, since that time, the foundation has distributed millions of dollars in grants, loans, and scholarships. Today, the Ford Foundation supports activities in all fifty states and in fifty different nations.[6]

Renaissance and Correcting Wrongs

Working with Detroit's first African American mayor, Coleman Young, Henry II also led the charge to build the Renaissance Center in downtown Detroit in the early 1970s, a $350 million hotel and office development located on the city's riverfront. The project was financed largely by the Ford company and other Detroit-based businesses that Henry II recruited.[7]

Henry Ford II also took steps to correct some of his grandfather's most serious missteps. After taking control of the company, he quickly fired Harry Bennett, who had been responsible for intimidating Ford employees and leading the brutal attacks against union organizers. He also tried to make amends to the Jewish community for his grandfather's remarks and support of anti-Semitic propaganda. He fired the editor responsible for the anti-Semitic articles that ran in the

Dearborn Independent. He also visited Israel in 1972, and in 1973, he sent Ford trucks to Israel to aid their cause in the Yom Kippur War. As a member of the exclusive Detroit Club, Ford II also worked to end their prohibition against accepting Jewish members.[8]

Ford's Successors

Henry Ford II served as Ford Company president until 1960. Since then, a series of leaders have helped steer Ford Motor Company through economic recessions, shortages in imported oil supply, and intense competition from foreign automakers. They have also developed new automobile platforms to satisfy changing consumer tastes, such as the Taurus sedan and the Explorer SUV.

In the 1990s, Alex Trotman from the United Kingdom, Ford's first foreign-born CEO, took steps to promote shared development and manufacturing across Ford's many worldwide companies to reduce costs and improve efficiency. More recently, in July 2018, Ford created a new division, Ford Autonomous Vehicles LLC, to further expand development of self-driving cars as well as taxi- and car-sharing services.

Challenges

Early in 2000, Henry Ford's great-grandson, CEO and Chairman of the Board William Clay Ford Jr., focused the company toward bigger vehicles just before gasoline prices jumped and consumers moved toward smaller cars that got better mileage. His successor, Alan Mulally, led efforts to reduce costs and sell nonessential companies that Ford had acquired

GOING HIGH-TECH

Automobiles have come a long way from the days of Henry Ford. While most cars still use internal combustion engines, they now produce much more power with fewer harmful emissions and better mileage than ever. The days of the internal combustion engine may soon be over, however. Major improvements in battery technology now allow today's electric vehicles (EVs) to travel more than 200 miles (322 km) before they have to be recharged, with even better performance on the horizon.

Just as Henry Ford was confronted with changing consumer tastes regarding style and comfort, many buyers today value the technology inside their cars as much as they value appearance and performance. Some features greatly improve safety, such as emergency braking, lane departure warning, and blind-side monitoring systems. Advanced applications now integrate drivers' mobile phones with their dashboards, turning today's automobiles into rolling entertainment centers, and some cars now even drive themselves. In his book, *The Great Race: The Global Quest for the Car of the Future*, author Levi Tillemann predicts that "the overwhelming odds are that the car of the future will [eventually] be less car than robot ... The transition to electric and driverless cars ... will change the way we live and many of the fundamentals of the global economy."[9]

The Ford Fusion hybrid (pictured) combined old and new technology by using a four-cylinder gasoline engine and a battery-powered electric motor to provide high fuel efficiency.

over the years, allowing Ford Motors to avoid the fate of competitors General Motors and Chrysler, which were forced to declare bankruptcy and accept US government bailout funds during the 2008 economic crisis.

Shocking Announcement

On Monday, May 22, 2017, Ford named James Hackett its tenth CEO. Less than one year later, in April 2018, Hackett turned heads by announcing a fundamental change in Ford

Ford CEO James Hackett in 2017. Automobile company leaders continue to face significant challenges as they try to address changes in technology and consumer tastes, as well as heightened concern about the effects of cars on the environment.

policy. Due to plunging demand and declining profits, Ford planned to discontinue making passenger cars and shift its resources to pickups, SUVs, and crossover vehicles, where sales were booming. "We're going to feed the healthy parts of our business and deal decisively with the areas that destroy value," Hackett said. "We're starting to understand what we need to do and making clear decisions there."[10]

Hackett's announcement may have appeared bold, but other manufacturers had also begun to reduce production and development of sedans and other passenger cars while expanding their choices of SUVs, crossovers, and pickup trucks. None went quite so far as Ford at first, but in November 2018, General Motors also announced a similar strategy.

The Road Continues

In many ways, Ford's radical shift in policy represented nothing more than another giant step on the path that its founder laid out more than one hundred years earlier. Henry Ford imagined a future where automobiles would connect every American with their neighbors and allow them to travel wherever and whenever they wanted. While technology may be changing in the twenty-first century, his company's mission remains true to Ford's original vision: make a better world through the design and manufacture of automobiles.

CHRONOLOGY

1863 Henry Ford is born in Dearborn, Michigan, on July 30.

1876 Henry Ford's mother dies in childbirth; Ford's desire to build self-propelled vehicles strengthens when he sees a steam-powered vehicle on a road near his house.

1879 Ford leaves his family farm to work in Detroit as a machinist.

1888 Henry Ford marries Clara Bryant.

1891 The Fords move to Detroit, and Henry begins working as an engineer at the Edison Illuminating Company.

1893 Ford's son Edsel is born on November 6; Ford builds his first successful gas-powered engine.

1896 Ford introduces his Quadricycle.

1899 Ford partners with investors to open the Detroit Automobile Company, which fails the next year.

1901 Ford starts the Henry Ford Company, which he later leaves; he also becomes American motor-racing champion.

1903 Henry Ford forms the Ford Motor Company on June 16.

1908 Ford's Model T goes into production.

1913 Ford begins using the moving assembly line at his plant.

1914 Ford more than doubles the daily wage to $5.

1918 The Model T becomes the best-selling car in the world; Henry Ford loses his bid for election to the United States Senate.

1919 Edsel Ford becomes president of Ford Motor Company, but his father remains in charge.

1927 The Model T ends production after slumping in 1926.

1937 Ford security guards attack organizers from the United Automobile Workers (UAW) during the "Battle of the Overpass."

1941 The UAW signs its first contract with the Ford Motor Company; the United States enters World War II; and Ford factories focus on war production.

1943 Edsel Ford dies at forty-nine years old, and Henry Ford comes out of retirement to become president of the company once again.

1945 Ford retires as his grandson Henry II becomes president of Ford Motor Company.

1947 Henry Ford dies at the age of eighty-three at his Dearborn home on April 7.

GLOSSARY

activist A person who believes strongly in political or social change and takes part in activities to accomplish his or her goals.

anti-Semitic Bias, hatred, or hostility against Jewish people.

assembly line A system that organizes workers and machines to put together parts of a product step by step to efficiently mass produce products.

budget A financial plan for a certain period of time.

consumer A person who buys goods and services.

conveyor belt A motorized chain or strip of flexible material that carries parts through a factory.

credit The ability of a customer to buy goods or services without paying immediately while promising to pay in the future.

forecasting Predicting or calculating the future using information from the past and the present.

foundry A factory where metal is melted and poured into molds to make objects.

Great Depression A time in US and world history when many people lost their jobs and lived in poverty (1929–1939).

horseless carriage Early description for automobiles, which replaced carriages pulled by horses.

incandescent lightbulb An object that produces light by the glow of a wire heated by electric current.

internal combustion engine An engine that gets its power from igniting a mixture of air and gasoline.

investor A person who puts their money into a company with the hope that they will make a profit when it becomes successful.

labor union A group of workers who join together to bargain with companies to get better wages or working conditions.

lawsuit A claim or complaint raised in a court of law.

libel A published false statement that damages a person's reputation.

mass production To make standardized products in large amounts.

pacifist A person who strongly opposes war.

parasite A person who takes advantage of others without giving anything in return.

patent A legal document that gives inventors ownership of their inventions and the right to use or sell them for a certain period of time.

peers People who are similar in age, ability, or social status .

profit A financial gain; the amount of money left over after costs and other expenses have been paid.

propaganda Information that is prepared and distributed to either help or hurt a person or cause.

sawmill A factory that saws logs into wooden boards.

self-propelled Something that can move itself.

shareholder A person who owns shares in a company and receives part of the company's profits and the right to vote on how the company is run (also called stockholders).

stroke A brain injury that occurs when a blood vessel that carries oxygen and nutrients to the brain is either blocked by a clot or bursts.

transmission The mechanism that transfers power from an automobile engine to the wheels.

trust A legal arrangement where someone's property or money is held or managed by someone else or by an organization.

turnover The rate at which people leave a company and are replaced by others.

vagabond A person who wanders from place to place without a job or a home.

vertical integration A business that produces all it needs from all levels without relying on outside sources.

SOURCES

INTRODUCTION

1. Russ Banham, *The Ford Century: Ford Motor Company and the Innovations that Shaped the World* (New York: Artisan, 2002), 30.

2. Ronald A. Reis, *Henry Ford For Kids: His Life and Ideas: With 21 Activities* (Chicago, IL: Chicago Review Press, 2016), 109.

CHAPTER ONE

1. "Industrial Revolution," History.com, Accessed September 23, 2018, https://www.history.com/topics/industrial-revolution/industrial-revolution.

2. Ibid.

3. "Economic Growth and the Early Industrial Revolution," US History online textbook, Accessed September 23, 2018, http://www.ushistory.org/us/22a.asp.

4. "The Industrial Revolution in the United States - Teacher Guide," Library of Congress: Teaching with Primary Sources, Accessed September 22, 2018, http://www.loc.gov/teachers/classroommaterials/primarysourcesets/industrial-revolution/pdf/teacher_guide.pdf.

5. Ibid.

6. Rebecca Beatrice Brooks, "The Industrial Revolution in America," History of Massachusetts blog, April 11, 2018, http://historyofmassachusetts.org/industrial-revolution-america.

7. Ibid.

8. Reis, *Henry Ford For Kids*, 1.

9. Rafael Tilton, *Henry Ford* (Farmington Hills, MI: Lucent Books, 2003), 20.

CHAPTER TWO

1. Carin T. Ford, *Henry Ford: The Car Man* (Berkeley Heights, NJ: Enslow Publishers, Inc., 2003), 8.

2. Don Mitchell, *Driven: A Photobiography of Henry Ford* (Washington, DC: National Geographic Society, 2010), 8.

3. Jeffrey Zuehlke, *Henry Ford* (Minneapolis, MN: Lerner Publications Company, 2007), 9.

4. Reis, *Henry Ford For Kids*, 3.

5. Mitchell, *Driven*, 8.

6. Michael Pollard, *Henry Ford: Auto Tycoon* (Farmington Hills, MI: Blackbirch Press, 2004), 10.

7. Michael Burgan, *Who Was Henry Ford?* (New York: Grosset & Dunlap, 2014), 19.

8. Ryan Nagelhout, *Henry Ford In His Own Words* (New York: Gareth Stevens Publishing, 2015), 9.

9. "Clara Bryant Ford, 1866–1950," Michigan Division Woman's National Farm & Garden Association, accessed September 13, 2018, https://michdivwnfga.weebly.com/clara-ford.html.

10. Burgan, *Who Was Henry Ford?*, 24.

11. Pollard, *Henry Ford: Auto Tycoon,* 16.

12. Burgan, *Who Was Henry Ford?*, 37.

13. Michael Burgan, *Henry Ford* (Milwaukee, WI: World Almanac Library, 2002), 18.

14. Pollard, *Henry Ford: Auto Tycoon,* 26–27.

15. Burgan, *Who Was Henry Ford?*, 65.

16. Haydn Middleton, *Henry Ford: The People's Carmaker* (New York: Oxford University Press, 1997), 22.

17. Banham, *The Ford Century*, 52.

18. Burgan, *Henry Ford*, 37.

19. Ibid., 43.

CHAPTER THREE

1. Sarah Colt, dir., *Henry Ford* (Boston, MA, WGBH, 2013), DVD.

2. Wayne G. Miller, *Car Crazy: The Battle for Supremacy Between Ford and Olds and the Dawn of the Automobile Age* (New York: PublicAffairs, 2015), xiii.

3. Mitchell, *Driven*, 17–18.

4. Nagelhout, *Henry Ford In His Own Words*, 22.

5. Colt, *Henry Ford*, DVD.

6. Miller, *Car Crazy*, xiv.

7. H. W. Brands, *Masters of Enterprise: Giants of American Business from John Jacob Astor and J. P. Morgan to Bill Gates and Oprah Winfrey* (New York: The Free Press, 1999), 102.

8. Burgan, *Henry Ford*, 33.

9. Colt, *Henry Ford*, DVD.

10. Anthony J. Mayo and Nitin Nohria, *In Their Time: The Greatest Business Leaders of the Twentieth Century* (Boston, MA: Harvard Business School Press, 2005), 68.

CHAPTER FOUR

1. Brands, *Masters of Enterprise*, 99.

2. Pollard, *Henry Ford: Auto Tycoon*, 20.

3. Reis, *Henry Ford For Kids*, 21.

4. Steven Roberts, *Henry Ford* (New York: The Rosen Publishing Group, Inc., 2013), 16.

5. Ford, *Henry Ford: The Car Man*, 23.

6. Burgan, *Who Was Henry Ford?*, 62–63, 65.

7. Pollard, *Henry Ford: Auto Tycoon*, 35.

8. Brands, *Masters of Enterprise*, 104.

9. Mayo and Nohria, *In Their Time*, 53.

10. Burgan, *Henry Ford*, 25.

11. Colt, *Henry Ford*, DVD.

12. Pollard, *Henry Ford: Auto Tycoon*, 4.

13. Ibid., 7.

14. Colt, *Henry Ford*, DVD.

15. Ibid.

16. Reis, *Henry Ford For Kids*, 35.

17. Colt, *Henry Ford*, DVD.

18. Burgan, *Henry Ford*, 27.

CHAPTER FIVE

1. Pollard, *Henry Ford: Auto Tycoon*, 9.

2. Zuehlke, *Henry Ford*, 7.

3. Ibid., 7.

4. Sheila Wyborny, *Henry Ford* (San Diego, CA: KidHaven Press, 2002), 11.

5. Burgan, *Henry Ford*, 41.

6. Colt, *Henry Ford*, DVD.

7. Jeff C. Young, *Henry Ford: Genius Behind the Affordable Car* (Berkeley Heights, NJ: MyReportLinks.com Books, 2008), 47.

8. Colt, *Henry Ford*, DVD.

9. Reis, *Henry Ford For Kids,* 38.

10. Colt, *Henry Ford*, DVD.

11. Ibid.

12. Banham, *The Ford Century*, 42.

13. Colt, *Henry Ford*, DVD.

14. Sean Braswell, "The Astonishing Ignorance of Henry Ford," Ozy, June 4, 2013, https://www.ozy.com/flashback/the-astonishing-ignorance-of-henry-ford/31368.

15. Burgan, *Who Was Henry Ford?*, 80.

16. Reis, *Henry Ford For Kids,* 59.

17. Nagelhout, *Henry Ford In His Own Words,* 10, 21.

18. Nagelhout, *Henry Ford In His Own Words*, 28.

19. Colt, *Henry Ford*, DVD.

CHAPTER SIX

1. Pollard, *Henry Ford: Auto Tycoon,* 36.

2. Mitchell, *Driven*, 6–7.

3. Burgan, *Henry Ford*, 6.

4. Jeffrey Vance, "Modern Times," Library of Congress, Accessed September 21, 2018, https://www.loc.gov/programs/static/national-film-preservation-board/documents/modern_times.pdf.

5. Mitchell, *Driven*, 40-41.

6. Young, *Henry Ford: Genius, 111.*

7. Banham, *The Ford Century*, 260.

8. Ibid., 102.

9. Levi Tillemann, *The Great Race: The Global Quest for the Car of the Future* (New York: Simon & Schuster, 2015), 6, 8.

10. Paul A. Eisenstein, "Ford to Stop Making All Passenger Cars Except the Mustang," NBC News, April 26, 2018, https://www.nbcnews.com/business/autos/ford-stop-making-all-passenger-cars-except-mustang-n869256.

FURTHER INFORMATION

BOOKS

Baime, A. J. *The Arsenal of Democracy: FDR, Detroit, and an Epic Quest to Arm an America at War.* Boston: Houghton Mifflin Harcourt, 2014.

Burns, Lawrence D., and Christopher Shulgan. *Autonomy: The Quest to Build the Driverless Car—And How It Will Reshape Our World.* New York: HarperCollins, 2018.

Ford, Henry, Samuel Crowther, and William A. Levinson. *The Expanded and Annotated My Life and Work: Henry Ford's Universal Code for World Class Success.* Boca Raton, FL: CRC Press, 2016.

Miller, G. Wayne. *Car Crazy: The Battle for Supremacy Between Ford and Olds and the Dawn of the Automobile Age.* New York: PublicAffairs, 2015.

Reis, Ronald A. *Henry Ford For Kids: His Life and Ideas: With 21 Activities.* Chicago: Chicago Review Press, 2016.

WEBSITES

Driving a Ford Model T Is a Lot Harder Than You'd Think! We Tried It
https://www.youtube.com/watch?v=MLMS_QtKamg

This video shows Bloomberg Pursuits' Hannah Elliott taking a 1914 Ford Model T for a spin after she receives a driving lesson to learn how to drive this complicated car.

Henry Ford: American Experience
https://www.pbs.org/wgbh/americanexperience/films/henryford

American Experience, an award-winning PBS series from WGBH Boston, features in-depth films about famous people and events that have shaped America's history. This website contains videos and articles about Henry Ford as well as scenes from the film that documents his life and influence.

Henry Ford's First Engine
https://www.youtube.com/watch?v=JKqU_sXyvUg

Students of Penn State University constructed this replica of Henry Ford's first "kitchen sink" engine, which he originally built in 1893. This video shows the engine in operation at the Henry Ford Museum/Greenfield Village during the Old Car Festival in 2014.

MUSEUM

The Henry Ford
20900 Oakwood Boulevard
Dearborn, MI 48124
313-982-6001

BIBLIOGRAPHY

Adolphus, David Traver. "The Inseparable, Irascible Dodge Boys." Hagerty, May 26, 2017. https://www.hagerty.com/articles-videos/articles/2017/05/26/dodge-brothers.

Banham, Russ. *The Ford Century: Ford Motor Company and the Innovations that Shaped the World.* New York: Artisan, 2002.

Brands, H.W. *Masters of Enterprise: Giants of American Business from John Jacob Astor and J. P. Morgan to Bill Gates and Oprah Winfrey.* New York: The Free Press, 1999.

Braswell, Sean. "The Astonishing Ignorance of Henry Ford." Ozy, June 4, 2013. https://www.ozy.com/flashback/the-astonishing-ignorance-of-henry-ford/31368.

Brooks, Rebecca Beatrice. "The Industrial Revolution in America." History of Massachusetts Blog, April 11, 2018. http://historyofmassachusetts.org/industrial-revolution-america.

Bryan, Ford R. "The Birth of the Henry Ford Company." The Henry Ford Heritage Association. Accessed September 17, 2018. http://hfha.org/the-ford-story/the-birth-of-ford-motor-company.

Burgan, Michael. *Who Was Henry Ford?* New York: Grosset & Dunlap, 2014.

Burgan, Michael. *Henry Ford*. Trailblazers of the Modern World. Milwaukee, WI: World Almanac Library, 2002.

"Clara Bryant Ford." Edisonfordwinterestates.org. Accessed September 13, 2018. http://www.edisonfordwinterestates. org/collections/biographies/clara-ford.

Colt, Sarah, dir. *Henry Ford*. American Experience. Boston, MA: WGBH, 2013. DVD.

"Economic Growth and the Early Industrial Revolution." US History online textbook. Accessed September 23, 2018. http://www.ushistory.org/us/22a.asp.

Eisenstein, Paul A. "Ford to Stop Making All Passenger Cars Except the Mustang." NBC News, April 26, 2018. https:// www.nbcnews.com/business/autos/ford-stop-making-all-passenger-cars-except-mustang-n869256.

Ford, Carin T. *Henry Ford: The Car Man.* Berkeley Heights, NJ: Enslow Publishers, Inc., 2003.

George, Bill. "Ford CEO Hackett's Decision to Dump Cars 'May Prove Fatal.'" CNBC, May 1, 2018. https://www. cnbc.com/2018/04/30/ford-ceo-jim-hacketts-decision-to-dump-cars-may-prove-fatal.html.

Hassler, William W., and Jennifer L. Weber. "American Civil War." *Encyclopædia Britannica*, August 23, 2018. https:// www.britannica.com/event/American-Civil-War

"Henry M. Leland." Automotive Hall of Fame. Accessed September 17, 2018. http://www.automotivehalloffame. org/honoree/henry-m-leland.

"A History of the Men Who Have Led Ford Motor Co." The Associated Press, May 22, 2017. https://apnews.com/ b6752b43f4ec4f0da47e0f6c1731297f.

Hoopes, James. "The Dehumanized Employee." CIO, February 4, 2005. https://www.cio.com.au/article/165305/ dehumanized_employee.

"Industrial Revolution." History.com. Accessed September 23, 2018. https://www.history.com/topics/ industrial-revolution/industrial-revolution.

"The Industrial Revolution in the United States - Teacher Guide." Library of Congress: Teaching with Primary Sources, accessed September 22, 2018. http://www.loc. gov/teachers/classroommaterials/primarysourcesets/ industrial-revolution/pdf/teacher_guide.pdf.

Mangan, Gregg. "Albert Augustus Pope, Transportation Pioneer." Connecticut History. Accessed September 18, 2018. https://connecticuthistory.org/albert-augustus-pope-1843-1909.

Mayo, Anthony J., and Nitin Nohria. *In Their Time: The Greatest Business Leaders of the Twentieth Century.* Boston, MA: Harvard Business School Press, 2005.

Middleton, Haydn. *Henry Ford: The People's Carmaker.* What's Their Story. New York: Oxford University Press, 1997.

Miller, Donald L. "The Industrial Age 1865 To 1917." American Heritage, November/December 2004. https://www.americanheritage.com/content/industrial-age-1865-1917.

Mitchell, Don. *Driven: A Photobiography of Henry Ford.* Washington, DC: National Geographic Society, 2010.

Nagelhout, Ryan. *Henry Ford in His Own Words.* Eyewitness to History. New York: Gareth Stevens Publishing, 2015.

Nolan, Jenny. "The Battle of the Overpass." *Detroit News*, August 6, 1997. http://blogs.detroitnews.com/history/1997/08/06/the-battle-of-the-overpass.

"Olds Motor Works Founded." History, August 21, 2018. https://www.history.com/this-day-in-history/olds-motor-works-founded.

Peterson-Withorn, Chase. "From Rockefeller to Ford, See Forbes' 1918 Ranking of the Richest People in America." Forbes, September 28, 2017. https://www.forbes.com/sites/chasewithorn/2017/09/19/the-first-forbes-list-see-who-the-richest-americans-were-in-1918/#3231c62e4c0d.

Pollard, Michael. *Henry Ford: Auto Tycoon.* Giants of American Industry. Farmington Hills, MI: Blackbirch Press, 2004.

Roberts, Steven. *Henry Ford, Jr.* Graphic American Inventors. New York: The Rosen Publishing Group, Inc., 2013.

"Thomas Edison." Biography.com, August 4, 2017. https://www.biography.com/people/thomas-edison-9284349.

Tillemann, Levi. *The Great Race: The Global Quest for the Car of the Future*. New York: Simon & Schuster, 2015.

Tilton, Rafael. *Henry Ford*. The Importance Of. Farmington Hills, MI: Lucent Books, 2003.

Vance, Jeffrey. "Modern Times." Library of Congress. Accessed September 21, 2018. https://www.loc.gov/programs/static/national-film-preservation-board/documents/modern_times.pdf.

"What Else Did Henry Ford Invent?" Infomedia, Accessed September 16, 2018. https://www.infomedia.com.au/what-else-did-henry-ford-invent.

Wyborny, Sheila. *Henry Ford*. Inventors and Creators. San Diego, CA: KidHaven Press, 2002.

Young, Jeff C. *Henry Ford: Genius Behind the Affordable Car*. Inventors Who Changed the World. Berkeley Heights, NJ: MyReportLinks.com Books, 2008.

Zuehlke, Jeffrey. *Henry Ford*. History Maker Bios. Minneapolis, MN: Lerner Publications Company, 2007.

INDEX

Page numbers in **boldface** refer to images.

activist, 41
agriculture, 10, 14, 17
anti-Semitic, 44, 86–87, 98, 100
assembly line, 6, 41, 45, 56, **64**, 65–66, 68–70, 73, 75, 94, 96, **97**

budget, 69, 83

Cadillac Automobile Company, 55–56, 58–59
Chevrolet, 58, 60
Civil War, 6, 9–10, 14, 16–17, 21, 24, 55
coal, 11, 39, 55, 76
consumer, 11, 63, 98, 101–102
conveyor belt, 68
cotton, 12, 14–16
cotton gin, **15**, 16
credit, 58, 63

Detroit, MI, 5, 21, 24–25, 28, 31–32, 36, 38–39, 46, 55–56, 58, 68, 76, 79, 94–96, 100
Detroit Automobile Company, 38
Dodge, John and Horace, 57–59, 67
Durant, William, 59–60

Edison, Thomas, **4**, 17, 32, **50**, 52, **53**, 54–55, 91
Edison Illuminating Company, 32, 36–37, 52, 54
Edison Institute, 89–90, 100
eight-hour workday, 41, 65, 73

factories, **8**, 12–14, 17, 20–21, 25, 41, 49, 68, 76, 83, 90, 96, 98
Ford, Clara, 18, **26**, 31–33, **33**, 36, 44, 48, 87
Ford, Edsel, 36, 45, 48, 56, 61, 88, **88**

Ford, Henry II, 33, 48, 93, 98, **99**, 100–101
Ford, Mary, 28–29, 33, 80, **81**
Ford, William, 27, 29
Ford Motor Company, **7**, 39, 45, 58, 61, 67, 88, 93–94, 101
forecasting, 69
foundry, 25

General Motors (GM), 56, 58–60, 63, 104–105
Great Britain, 9–13, 16
Great Depression, 45
Greenfield Village, 89–91, **90**

horseless carriage, 6, 18, 32, 38, 54

immigrants, 17, 21, 59, 76
incandescent lightbulb, 54
Industrial Revolution, 5, 10, 14, 17–18, 96
internal combustion engine, 18, 31–32, 52, 94, 102
investor, 13, 38–40, 47, 55–56, 58, 61, 81, 84, 86, 93
iron, 11, 25, 31, 76

labor union, 46–47
lawsuit, 59–60
libel, 85, 87

Lincoln Motor Company, 56, 58, 88

mass production, 96
migration, 17
Model T, **4**, 6, **39**, 40–41, 45, 52, 61, 63, 65, 69, 73–76, **74**, 83–85, 87, 89
monopoly, 60

Oldfield, Barney, **34–35**, 39
Olds, Ransom, 52, 56–57
Oldsmobile, 52, 56, 58–60
outwork system, 13

pacifist, 41
parasite, 84
patent, 16, 60, 66
peers, 66
profit, 15–16, 20, 38, 40, 46, 59, 66, 70, 72–73, 84, 104
propaganda, 100

Quadricycle, 36, **37**

railroads, 6, 13, 17, 20, 24, 76
River Rouge, 41, **42–43**, 47, 90–91, 94
rural, 21, 28, 30, 79, 85–86, 90, 95–96

sawmill, 25

self-propelled, 18, 23, 36
shareholder, 40, 59
steam engine, 6, 12–13, 18,
    30–32, 52
steel, 11, 17, 20, 36, 40, 75
stockholders, 45, 59, 84
stroke, 48

tariffs, 20
textiles, **8**, 11, 16
tobacco, 14
transcontinental railroad, 17
transmission, 66–67

trust, 20
turnover, 71, 73

United Automobile Workers
    (UAW), 46–48
urban, 21

vagabond, 55
vertical integration, 70

Whitney, Eli, 16
World War I, 41, 46
World War II, 98

ABOUT THE AUTHOR

Gerry Boehme is a published author, editor, speaker, and business consultant who loves to travel and to learn about new things. Boehme has written books for students dealing with many subjects, including *Spying, Surveillance, and Privacy in the Twenty-First Century: Edward Snowden: Heroic Whistle-Blower or Traitorous Spy?*, *Primary Sources of the Civil Rights Movement: John Lewis and Desegregation*, *Public Persecutions: Heresy: The Spanish Inquisition*, and *Getting to Broadway: How Hamilton Made It to the Stage*. He was born in New York City, graduated from the Newhouse School at Syracuse University, and now lives on Long Island with his wife and two children. His first car was a Ford.